Front cover:
Novyi Vavilon (The New Babylon, Sovkino, 1929). Kozintsev and Trauberg's film was sold to German audiences as a Prussian national epic, with disastrous results. (page 182).

This issue:
Non-Fiction Film

Edited by Mark Langer

Editorial office:

Richard Koszarski
Box TEN
Teaneck, New Jersey, 07666, USA
E-mail: filmhist@aol.com

Publishing office:

John Libbey & Company Pty Ltd
Level 10, 15–17 Young Street
Sydney, NSW 2000
Australia
Telephone: +61 (0)2 9251 4099
Fax: +61 (0)2 9251 4428
E-mail: jlsydney@mpx.com.au

Other offices:

John Libbey & Company Ltd
13 Smiths Yard, Summerley Street
London SW18 4HR, UK
Telephone: +44 (0)181-947 2777
Fax: +44 (0)1-947 2664

John Libbey Eurotext Ltd, Montrouge, France
John Libbey - CIC s.r.l., Rome, Italy

Printed in Australia by
Gillingham Printers Pty Ltd, South Australia

CW00496087

An International Journal

Volume 9, Number 2, 1997

This issue:
NON-FICTION FILM

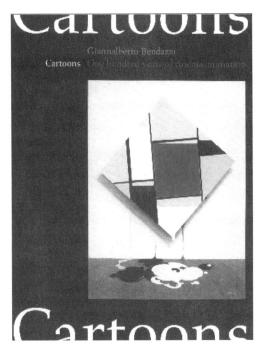

Film History, Volume 9, pp. 131–131, 1997. Copyright © John Libbey & Company
ISSN: 0892-2160. Printed in Australia

Non-fiction film

The term 'non-fiction film' encompasses a broad range of cinema, which has been widened considerably by contemporary scholarship. As examined in this issue of *Film History*, the term includes not only traditional documentaries and newsreels, but also such diverse forms as films made for television broadcast and animation.

Various perspectives on the history of non-fiction film are presented in this issue.

Gene Walz's interview with veteran National Film Board (NFB) of Canada producer Ches Yetman not only documents the filmmaker's career in the context of Canadian film production, but engages with the practical considerations of changing forms of dissemination of non-fiction films, questions of regionalism within Canadian cinema and the history of the NFB.

Charles Wolfe's examination of voice-over narration interrogates previous accounts of the history of this convention through a consideration of a variety of strategies used in early American sound documentaries, and explores issues related to the means by which critics and historians describe the commentator's voice in documentary film. Among the issues that Wolfe explores are the relations between the sound and visual texts of voice-over documentaries. Wolfe centres his study on the films *The Spanish Earth* (1937) and *The Battle of Midway* (1942).

In keeping with *Film History*'s policy of publishing articles that do not conform directly to the major theme of the issue, this collection includes the results of Thomas Saunders' research into the ill-fated German–Soviet business venture called the *Deutsch-Russische-Film-Allianz*, better known by its acronym Derussa. In the context of film production in Germany during the late silent period, Saunders outlines the brief history of this film company from its conception to its sensational collapse.

Perhaps one of the most neglected areas of investigation in the realm of non-fiction film is the animated documentary. Sybil DelGaudio, in her consideration of animated documentary in relation to current theoretical literature on non-fiction film, points out the problematic nature inherent in the study of an area of non-fiction film that does not mechanically reproduce a pro-filmic event. Likening the animated documentary to such forms as the re-enactment film, or more technologically mediated media that call into question long-held beliefs about the ontological nature of the photographic image, DelGaudio gives a brief survey of American animated documentaries as a prelude to a closer examination of the films of John and Faith Hubley.

Recent years have seen a dramatic expansion of television non-fiction forms, both on broadcast and speciality cable systems. Jason Mittell's article on the early television series *Industry on Parade* deals with non-fiction television both in regard to its debt to the sponsored film and in regard to the overlap between film and the new broadcast medium in the 1950s. Produced on film but disseminated primarily on television, *Industry on Parade* serves as a vehicle through which Mittell examines such issues as the role of a television text for historians, canon formation, and the effect of the canon on the priorities of archival preservation. ♣

Mark Langer

Film History, Volume 9, pp. 132–148, 1997. Copyright © John Libbey & Company
ISSN: 0892-2160. Printed in Australia

The NFB is a state of mind: An interview with Ches Yetman

Gene Walz

The National Film Board of Canada has spent much of its nearly 60-year existence reinventing itself. Founded by an act of Parliament in May 1939, the NFB or the Film Board – as it is more familiarly known – quickly established itself as a world-class propaganda-maker during World War II. Since then its mission has never been as urgent or, for some, as clear. To show Canada to Canadians and Canadians to the rest of the world has not been enough to sustain its early momentum or justify its demands on the public purse.

In the 1950s, aided by new light-weight equipment, much of it developed within its own walls, the NFB led the way in direct cinema or cinéma vérité documentaries. Unit B, comprised of Tom Daly, Roman Kroitor, Colin Low, Wolf Koenig, and Stanley Jackson, completed a series of films that gave Canada international fame and influence.[1] Films such as *Paul Tomkowicz* (1954), *City of Gold* (1957), *Corral* (1954), *Universe* (1960) and *Lonely Boy* (1961) stand out. A network of distribution officers not only made sure that these films were seen by Canadians; they also circulated new film ideas back to production headquarters.

By the mid-1960s this reciprocal process was found wanting. So the Challenge for Change/Société nouvelle program was initiated, spurred on by respected filmmaker Colin Low. It was designed to provide the NFB's equipment and the expertise of its filmmakers to the disadvantaged citizens of Ca-

nada's far-flung communities, most notably to Fogo Island, Newfoundland. The objective of the Challenge for Change program was outlined by Low himself:

> The means of communication – real two-way communication – must be made accessible to ordinary people for dialogue in meaningful local debate. In this way, we would generate a much more vigorous problem-solving capacity based upon local initiative and creativity.[2]

The initial success of this program was instrumental in creating another NFB revitalising program – the regionalisation of the NFB's production funds and facilities. Filmmaker Peter Jones was dispatched to Vancouver, British Columbia in 1965 to set up a regional production centre there. Many were skeptical about its value and nervous about its negative effects on the NFB's Montreal centre; some even feared that it was not just a dispersal of talent but a dismantling of the operation of the Film Board. Jones provided a succinct answer to those who required a justification for regionalised filmmaking.

Gene Walz is head of the Film Studies Program at the University of Manitoba. His book *Canada's Greatest Films* is currently in press (Rodopi). Correspondence: 450 University College, University of Manitoba, Winnipeg, Manitoba, Canada R3T 2M8.

Because Canada is 3,827 miles wide. Because, for all the efforts of the CBC [Canadian Broadcasting Corporation – for radio and television], the NFB, the CNR [Canadian National Railroad] and Air Canada, for all the telephones and teletypes, newspapers, magazines, and books – for all these methods of communication – there is still a huge gulf in realities and attitudes between Canadians of the different regions. Because with the best intentions in the world, we cannot sense the current mood of a region, or always even detect the essence of a film subject, by making periodic research and shooting excursions throughout the country.[3]

Despite this proselytising, regionalisation did not become a reality until 1972 when the Pacific Regional Production Centre was securely established in Vancouver. Within three years an Atlantic Centre was opened in Halifax, Nova Scotia, a Prairie Centre in Winnipeg, Manitoba, and an Ontario Centre in Toronto, Ontario. In 1980 a Northwest Centre was set up in Edmonton, Alberta. These centres had to contend with central office recalcitrance and never-adequate budgets, but they quickly provided fresh, intimate, unique new films for the NFB's inventory; they also supported local film cooperatives and jump-started regional production companies. The obvious success of regionalisation could be measured in many ways.

From the beginning the Prairie Production Centre was different from its sister studios, if for no other reason than the fact that it was the most difficult to staff. Because of its severe winters and its isolation, filmmakers were reluctant to be transferred from comfortable Montreal to forbidding Winnipeg. Thus, the first two executive producers of the Prairie Region were hometown boys returning to their roots. In fact, their local knowledge and contacts gave new producers Jerry Krepakevitch and Michael Scott a decided advantage over the other regional centres. Not only did the Prairie office complete films quicker, it was the first one to make documentary films as well as animation and fiction films. By the time Ches Yetman replaced Scott as executive producer for the Prairie Region in 1985, NFB films made there had already won several Canadian Film Awards, one had been nomi-

nated for an Academy Award in Hollywood for Best Animation (*The Big Snit*, 1985), and one had been accepted at the Cannes Film Festival (*Ted Baryluk's Grocery*, 1983).[4]

Yetman's route to the position of executive producer can only be described as circuitous, clichéd though that term may be. Born in Newfoundland before it was a part of Canada, Yetman began his NFB employment as a distribution officer in the Maritime provinces in 1965. He quickly established a reputation as a clever promoter of NFB films and then as an eager participant in the Challenge for Change/Société nouvelle program.

By 1972 he had landed a job in the head office in Montreal as a special projects coordinator in the Media Research Division. It was here that he rubbed elbows with the NFB's most prestigious filmmakers, consulting regularly with Tom Daly and especially Donald Brittain, two of the most influential figures in the NFB's history.[5] As a liaison officer, he also met with many of the best of the world's filmmakers to screen their films and exchange ideas. In addition to this, he was responsible for launching films and for explicating some of the more experimental works being encouraged then.

In 1978 he moved with his wife and family to Winnipeg where he became Regional Marketing Coordinator for the West. It was in this position that he solidified his reputation as an imaginative promoter. He advertised Prairie NFB films on matchbooks, mugs, paper bags, postcards, pens, T-shirts, and sweatshirts. He was responsible for creating an enviable series of eye-catching posters. And he established the first NFB boutique where all these items could be purchased.

When Mike Scott left in 1985, Yetman replaced him as executive producer, the first non-filmmaker to be appointed to such a position. As executive producer he continued the practice started by Scott of producing animation, fiction and documentary films. Noteworthy credits include *The Cat Came Back* (1988), which garnered over 19 international awards including an Oscar nomination for Best Animation, *The Apprentice* (1991) and *La Salla* (1996). He also produced the Prairie NFB's first fiction feature film *The Outside Chance of Maximilian Glick* (1987), as well as *The Last Winter* (1989), *Bordertown Cafe* (1991), and *For the Moment* (1994). Probably his finest accomplishment

THE NATIONAL FILM BOARD OF CANADA
PRESENTS

FAT CHANCE
is the funny and sensitive story of
Rick Zakowich who started on a diet to lose
half his body weight and found all of himself
along the way. Rick's journey is to a new identity.
In the process of discovery, he finds himself moving
towards a destination he could not have anticipated.
Values, assumptions and perspectives are
turned inside out; where fat may be the issue
but difference is the ultimate truth.

Length: 72 : 20

PHOTOGRAPHY: ROBERT BARROW   DESIGN: LILAC STUDIO/TOOTS

FAT CHANCE
THE BIG PREJUDICE

DIET CENTRE

RICK ZAKOWICH
CHARLES KONOWAL, C.S.C.
NORMAN DUGAS, LEON JOHNSON   IAN HODGES
BONNIE DICKIE   RUSS DYCK, KEN GREGORY
SCOTT COLLINS
CYNDI FORCAND
ANNA MARIE BOQUIST
CHES YETMAN
JOE MacDONALD, CHARLES KONOWAL
JEFF McKAY

VHS
C 9194 042

Closed captioned

This video is cleared for public performance providing no entry fee charged. Unauthorized
duplication, cablecast or broadcast is a violation of Canadian copyright laws.
© 1994 National Film Board of Canada P.O. Box 6100, Station Centre-Ville, Montreal, Quebec H3C 3H5
Printed in Canada

Fig. 1. Striking graphics were always a priority for Yetman.

was the series *Daughters of the Country* (1987), four one-hour fiction films based on the personal confrontations between aboriginal women and Euro-Canadian culture. It had the most elaborate marketing plan of any NFB production to that point and met with international success.

As a producer of documentaries Yetman has favoured portrait documentaries over other kinds, but they have been extraordinarily varied in their choice of subjects. Among them, there are conventional portraits of a beloved Prairie politician (*Tommy Douglas: Keeper of the Flame*, 1986), a renowned Royal Winnipeg Ballet dancer (*Moment of Light: The Dance of Evelyn Hart*, 1994), and a Ukrainian-Canadian sculptor (*Leo Mol: In Light and Shadow*, 1993). At the other extreme are feature-length portraits of an inventor intent on almost single-handedly building a new fighter for the Air

Force (*The Defender*, 1989), a street kid who is HIV-positive and was adopted by a gay city-councillor (*A Kind of Family*, 1992), an obese man in search of an effective weight-loss program (*Fat Chance*, 1994), and a former hooker fighting substance abuse (*The True Story of Linda M.*, 1995).

If there is a consistent thread to his work as a producer of documentaries, it is based on the fact that most of his films focus on 'lost causes'. Tommy Douglas is one of the patron saints of a party (the New Democrats) that has never held national power; Bob Diemert is unable to build a fighter plane to his own requirements, much less the government's; the street kid ends up in serious trouble again with the law; the fat man can't lose weight, and the ex-prostitute can't shake her alcohol and drug dependency. Even the title animal in *Return of the Swift Fox* (1988) is having trouble in its reintroduction to its former Prairie habitat. Like the main character in Yetman's favourite film, Donald Brittain's *Volcano: An Inquiry into the Life and Death of Malcolm Lowry* (1976), the subjects of his own documentaries are not successful in their endeavours.

Yet there is something noble about these people throughout the films, something redeeming in their portraits. Likely this is because his films never present the characters as foolish or pitiable. As a producer he has insisted that his portraits present complex individuals in all of their humanity. Often amusing but never trivialised, his characters are also at times pathetic, yet they are never demeaned. His films cut to the heart of voice and audience issues in documentary practice, issues that the NFB has debated for almost 60 years. Who are documentaries made for, and why?

Yetman has also been secure enough to allow the one veteran documentary director in his employ, John Paskievich, to develop his own style and pursue his own peculiar interests – from old-world fundamentalists living in Alberta (*The Old Believers*, 1988), to Inuit marble-sculptors (*Sedna: The*

Fig. 2. Peabody Award-winning producer Ches Yetman prior to leaving the NFB in 1996.

Making of Myth, 1992), to weekend warriors in central Europe (*If Only I Were an Indian*, 1995). Paskievich has won many awards, as has Yetman – including the highly prestigious Peabody Award in 1995 for *Fat Chance*.

Honours mean little in a precarious economy, however. In 1996, faced with a continually shrinking budget, the NFB moved to once again reinvent itself. Yetman was one of the unlucky veteran employees 'surplussed' by the NFB. He left its employ in May 1996 and now works for a Winnipeg production company. His first film in his new capacity as a non-NFB producer was on the Avro Aero jet, a promotional film shown on television just before

the two-part mini-series depicting the demise of that ill-fated aeroplane. His future plans include promotion and distribution as well as producing.

Yetman was interviewed in two sessions by Gene Walz. The interviews were edited together.

G.W. What's the difference between producing an NFB documentary and an NFB drama?

C.Y. In producing a drama you spend a lot more time trying to work out the financing and the organisational logistics of the production. Documentary is more intimate. You can start with an idea and work with it all the way through. Drama, once you've settled on a script and worked out the logistics, is pretty straightforward. Construction work. It's not as creatively demanding. It might not be easy to do, but it's like following a blueprint.

I found in working on dramas, that there were far more egos involved, a million people and each one, it seemed, needed some tending to. In documentaries you have a very small crew; you can work more closely with them and have more input.

Animation is the most intimate of all. I used to joke that we should do nothing but animation.

On the other hand, when you're working on the kinds of documentaries that we did, you're not only dealing with the crew and the creative end of things, you also have to deal with the people being filmed. When you do films like *The True Story of Linda N.* or *Fat Chance*, your subjects can get pissed off at things. On documentaries like these, there is *always* conflict, even if the projects start smoothly. Differences of opinion develop between the subjects and the director. As executive producer you have to resolve these conflicts. You're always trying to make sure you get the best possible movie out of all of this. But the people who are being filmed have other agendas. It's not just changing lines or line-readings; it's much more disruptive than that.

Then again when you make any kind of movie in Canada, whether it's documentary or drama or animation, you always have the same thing to worry about: how am I going to get audiences to see this film?

G.W. What is your opinion about the current state of documentaries in Canada?

C.Y. One of the big problems that has developed with documentaries is the result of changes at CBC television's *The Journal* and *The National*.[6] I think the CBC has given documentary a bad name. They no longer call a piece they do on *The Journal* a 'public affairs' piece. They've started calling it a documentary. All of a sudden documentaries got associated in the public mind with public affairs. So the whole idea that a documentary had a point of view became less important. *The Journal* would have a talking head come on camera to set things up; all the rest would be straight information done in voice-over – and it wasn't really a documentary.

A documentary is supposed to be something with a clear point of view. You might not agree with that point of view, but at least you're very clear what it is. A documentary does not try to find any balance; it's pretty subjective. It tries to make you agree with

its argument, or at least it certainly provokes you. That's what the best documentaries do. Provocation is what they're all about.

A public affairs piece may look at the same topic but it tries to provide some balance. Even though it may have a point of view, it tries to include the other side to make sure that nobody's going to criticise the filmmakers for being biased. And they pretend that somehow they're objective.

G.W. Has the NFB also been in the business of making public affairs pieces lately?

C.Y. I think what's happened is that about ten years ago, when Peter Katadotis became director of the Film Board, it got really pre-occupied with social issues and then started to pursue this new genre. The filmmakers decided to take on alcoholism or spousal abuse or whatever, and what happened was they got very earnest about making sure that the public knew about the issues involved. In the process of focussing on content too much, they lost their ability to focus on good filmmaking as well.

G.W. Isn't *Fat Chance* about a social issue?

C.Y. In *Fat Chance* there's a social concern, yes, but at the same time there are ideas and techniques that go back to the Studio C or Unit B era.[7] If you look at it again, *Lonely Boy* (1962) is a social issue film in a sense.[8] But its audience stays with it because it's an interesting subject matter done in a new and very fascinating way. When the Board moved into that deep social concern phase ten years ago, it lost part of the tradition of being innovators.

G.W. So, the NFB isn't 'cutting edge' anymore? There are not enough risk-takers?

C.Y. Even though the Film Board over the years emphasised the fact that they wanted to take risks, they became very nervous when the risks were too big. When you try to challenge the accepted forms, you take a huge risk because the chances of its failing are so much bigger.

G.W. What risks did you take as an executive producer?

C.Y. *Fat Chance* was the biggest risk. It's the kind of film that we could have approached in two ways. One way to approach it was to go to somebody's nutritionist and talk to him on camera about this subject matter and then string a series of statements together. What you get is a one-hour public affairs-style documentary that deals with the question of

Fig. 3. The two fat people: *Fat Chance's* Rick Zacowich and friend (Before and After).

obesity and related matters. But it doesn't create any empathy for an individual who is fat. If the audience is looking at it, the first response to this standard, traditional approach would be to just process the information. But they'll have no affiliation or feeling towards what the whole experience would be.

To me it was a big risk because we didn't know where we were gonna go with it. We didn't know what to expect. What if the guy didn't lose 400 pounds? What if along the way he decides this is too hard on him emotionally and he doesn't want to continue to participate? That happens. He could easily see the project as manipulative or as just too much of a strain on him and then bail out.

To complicate things, the subject and the director had conflicts. There were also conflicts between the director and the producers. And the whole structure of the film, not just the subject matter, became like a piece of research. As a producer I needed to know all those things about nutrition and all those other factors. I had to find that out. But when it comes to an audience participating in the process, they don't need to know all that. The real issue is that people who are fat are discriminated against. That's what you want to communicate. You could communicate that through a series of testimonials, but you wouldn't have very many people watching it.

The reason it was so successful is because it had [interesting people and interesting conflicts] rather than useful information you felt you had to get across. It was different.

G.W. What made you move in that direction?

C.Y. Over the past five or six years I started to think about the audience a lot more. When I watched lots of documentaries on television or wherever, I was really bored. I never quite knew whom they were pitched at.

There's an enormous, enormous audience out there that never watches documentaries. They're somewhere between the ages of 15 and 25 and they rarely read a newspaper. When they watch TV, they certainly don't watch the news. And their favourite television channel is HBO – though I have found out that they do watch some documentaries there, which is interesting. So I got in touch with HBO in New York and they gave me, like, 20 documentaries. And they were great.

They're not like *The Journal* or *Dateline* or *60 Minutes*. They're entertaining. I remember one in particular that was set in Little Rock, Arkansas. It was an hour-long documentary on street gangs. It started off at the Governor's Mansion. Two blocks down from the mansion is the largest concentration of street gangs per capita of any place in America. Now normally somebody would interview a cop and a social worker and they'd go 'yadda, yadda, yadda'. What these people did was get inside the gang and tell it from there.

Entertainment is a really important part of HBO's documentary approach. The strange thing is that ordinarily if you use the word 'entertainment', people think of it as frivolous because documentary is supposed to be serious, earnest, the socially conscious thing to do. But if you want to reach the unreached, you're going to have to do it by entertaining them in really innovative ways. They'll get the message, but they don't want to be preached at.

I sometimes thought that all documentaries by the Film Board or on television had a certain target audience and they were all my age [over 50]. Some of the older Film Board documentaries I was pleased with because they seemed to reach out to a younger audience, and I've always been interested in the younger audience. There's a bigger challenge to it.

G.W. Is that what attracted you to *A Kind of Family*?

C.Y. That had an appeal to a younger audience because it had a young guy that kids could identify with. He was a kid on the edge and every kid could identify with what that kid went through. Maybe not to the same extent. But it also had a wide appeal to a non-traditional documentary audience.

G.W. Non-traditional is a good way to describe your whole career. How did you originally get started in film?

C.Y. Many, many years ago I had a sister-in-law who worked for the Film Board in St. John's, Newfoundland. They used to run films every Wednesday night and she got me to go watch them. I found it fascinating that films could be made about people and things I could relate to. And then a job came up in distribution there that I applied for and didn't get. About three months later, I was offered the same

job in Halifax. I had never been out of Newfoundland so this seemed like a big deal to go to Halifax as a distribution officer.

My job was the strangest job you could imagine. At that time the Board had pink cards which people had to fill out for each film that was shown; we had to keep track of when and where the film was shown, and how many people saw it. Every month I had to send those cards in to the head office in Montreal. Your performance, I soon realised, was judged by the number of pink cards you sent in.

I think I ran pink cards out of the Film Board. What happened was, I got the brilliant idea of starting a film circuit in Halifax with the fire department. I would supply each firehall with a projector and a package of films. Each firehall had three shifts a day; there were twenty firehalls in the city. The firemen had nothing else to do but watch movies. They'd even truck them on to the next place for me. Just from the firehalls alone, I would end up with something like a thousand screenings a month. It was way beyond what anybody else in the country was doing. So then I think the Film Board decided to get out of the pink card business. Although I stayed only six months, I think by the time I left Halifax, every fireman had seen every NFB film ever made.

G.W. Did you do the same thing at your next post?

C.Y. I soon got bored with that side of things. In St. John, New Brunswick I got involved with the Challenge for Change program using portapacks with black and white videotape. I spent four years, 1968 to 1972, working on that.

We made videos on social issues like poverty or housing problems. We'd sit some people down and get them talking about bad housing. We'd videotape it and then take the videotape next door and show it to the neighbours. Then we'd videotape them talking about their bad housing. And so on. Eventually we had the whole south-end of St. John on videotape talking about bad housing.

As a result of this, people began to organise. So we edited all the bad-housing footage down to a half hour or so, and we took it to city council. And then we videotaped the city council's response to the bad-housing videotape. And so on. It was really pretty satisfying.

G.W. You eventually made it to the NFB's head office in Montreal.

C.Y. That's when I got involved with the esoteric, with the world of media. The Film Board set up a program called Media Research. We would do seminars and workshops and six-week institutes or exchanges. We'd bring people to the NFB from all over the world, people like Buckminster Fuller, Fred Wiseman, The Maysles brothers – all these amazing characters.[9] That part of my job motivated me the most because I wanted to meet these guys. Well, when we brought in Fred Wiseman, Guy Glover was just ecstatic.[10] It was unreal. We screened everything Wiseman ever made and then we had three days of sessions. It was a training thing, to learn about the latest things that were going on. And I remember saying to Guy after it was all over, 'You know, Fred Wiseman's stuff is all the same. It has the same style.' And he looked at me and he said, 'Well, at least he has style'. We were much more interested in style then.

G.W. You did a book on Don Brittain. Was he a big influence on you back then?

C.Y. I don't think he was. I knew him fairly well and we worked together a lot over the years. My involvement with him began at the launching of *Volcano* across Canada and the United States. I had to help promote the film despite the fact that the Film Board people didn't think it was very good. I was involved in the film from pretty close to the beginning and Don was wonderful because at every stage, at every cut, he would bring me in. But I was the worst person to bring in because he once showed me a two-and-a-half-hour version that I thought was fantastic. I didn't see anything at all wrong with it. He felt that no one was going to watch a two-and-a-half-hour documentary on a writer.

Later a colleague of mine and I organised a screening of *Volcano*, the final rough-cut, and I had the NFB people come up to me horrified and ask: 'What in the world are we going to do with this? It's just basically a film about a drunk.' But I thought it was a film about everything. Not just about this writer but about a person's conflicts, about his dark side. It had everything. It was a big film for me.

But Brittain wasn't the major influence. It was Tom Daly. When I first got to Montreal, I came to know him really, really well and he was a great teacher, very precise. And he represented the house style there at the time. I can remember Mike Rubbo telling me once that the thing he dreaded most was

to have to sit down and talk to Daly after a new film of his was assembled. Daly used to have a small clipboard with a light on it, and he'd go into a screening and he could look at the film and write his notes without taking his eyes off the screen. He wrote enormous amounts of notes on every film. He'd end up with 30 or 40 pages of notes. And then the director had to sit down and discuss his notes with him. Well, it wasn't a discussion about generalities. I was a part of those discussions, and they were all on specifics. It went like this. Tom would say, 'You know that shot near the opening. I think there's a better shot than that one. Remember that shot where the bird goes from left to right and then just hovers there? That one would be better there.' And Mike Rubbo used to hate that. He said it was like going back to being a university student for every film. And it wasn't like you were there for an hour; it was for four or six hours.[11]

Sad Song of Yellow Skin (1970). That was Tom Daly's idea to put Rubbo into the film. He didn't find the first cut of the film all that interesting. It was Tom Daly who found snippets of Rubbo on film and recommended that he impose himself on the structure of the film. Tom was very good at that. He was like the NFB's film doctor.

G.W. Do you think Daly is the unacknowledged godfather of the NFB?

C.Y. I always thought he was. He was so interesting. He was there from the beginning, and he was a scholar. I mean he had a scholarly view of the world. It wasn't like let's just get it done and on TV. He had a more philosophical view of what he was doing. So it wasn't just a question of discussing a shot from the point of view of whether it worked technically. It was more philosophical. He was very good at honing in on what the central theme and issues of a documentary film were. Everything else didn't matter.

He was never really critical. He would sit there and tell you something, and you kind of went away thinking that he was on your side. But he would remind you that you had to be a good storyteller. Otherwise all you get is just a lot of 'stuff' and then it's tough to try to make a story out of it. Lots of people say that a documentary is made in the editing room, but he would say that if you start off telling a good story in an entertaining way, then that's half the battle.

G.W. Were any of your Manitoba film projects vetted with Daly?

C.Y. No. He was gone before I started producing. In fact, he was the guy who told me never to go into producing and I think there was some truth in what he said.

G.W. Why was that?

C.Y. Well, when I was leaving Montreal to come to Manitoba, I had a choice: leave the Film Board or come to Winnipeg, basically. Before I left Montreal, I sought Tom Daly's counsel. He gave me some very interesting advice. He said 'If you don't know more than the director, you shouldn't be a producer'. There's a great deal of truth to that. If you're a producer, you've got to be able to bring something to the table on an intellectual level that's greater than what the director brings. That's not to be pretentious or self-important or anything. You've got to know the subject matter and how documentaries work in terms of structure, etc. And Tom Daly certainly did! He knew more than any director that ever worked at the Film Board – including Don Brittain. In fact, Brittain only took advice on his films from two people at the board – Guy Glover and Tom Daly. That was it. Those were the only people he would really listen to.

G.W. Why Guy Glover?

C.Y. He was the same kind of prof as Tom Daly. If you sat down with Tom and Guy, at the end of the day, it was not about filmmaking but about fairly large worldly issues. And Guy took the long view. That's why he was against video. It had nothing whatsoever to do with an antagonism to the new technology. He was really into the new technologies. He wasn't against them at all. The reason he was against video was because the image just wasn't very good. He thought of the Film Board in terms of someone looking at the images one hundred years from now. When he brought his producers together to look at the films, it was to ask questions about whether someone would want to watch it 20 years from now or in the year 2065. That was the reason he didn't want video. He saw film as the archives of the culture. And it's true. After seven years or so, the video images will be gone.

G.W. Is there anybody like Guy at the Film Board these days? Are people still brought in?

C.Y. No, not really. That was the golden age of the Film Board. The 1960s and 1970s. It was pretty

much gone by 1980. There aren't the kind of mentors like Tom and Guy were back then, though Don Haig is sort of like that. He's done a really good job since he returned to Studio C about three or four years ago.[12]

G.W. Well, Colin Low is still there. He's been there for 50 years, hasn't he?

C.Y. Yeah, he's from the same school. They all liked to argue. They believed in the idea of creative tension. Tom Daly brought in Derek May and Richard Raxlen and Robin Spry, about six or seven new people.[13] And all they did was fight with the older people. And out of it came some very different things. Tom was always interested in different approaches. He'd produce a one-hour documentary and then he'd produce experimental films by Derek May. Guy Glover produced *Angel* (1966) – a beautiful film with very strange imagery, and I don't see that kind of thing going on there now.

Don Brittain recognised the problem years ago. He said it was very difficult for film to survive at the Film Board when the filmmakers aren't in charge. And that's what's happening now. People who really, deep down, don't have a love of film are running the place.

G.W. Do you mean right from the very top down?

C.Y. Even that has changed dramatically over the years. When I joined the Film Board, the film commissioner was Guy Roberge. He was an odd man, but he talked directly to the prime minister, Lester Pearson. Being the film commissioner then was like being a minister in the federal cabinet. That's the role Grierson played, and his successor Ross McLean. When McLean was mad, he wouldn't talk to an assistant deputy minister; he went right to the Prime Minister, who was a friend of his. If he thought he was being squished, he let the guy at the top know about it.

Over the years the film commissioner moved from that kind of situation to a more bureaucratic and administrative role where he or she reported to a deputy minister. So the process is now quite different. The film commissioner no longer barks right at the prime minister: 'You can't do this to me and my people'. Grierson and McLean and Roberge were formidable enemies to have if you were prime minister.

Hugo McPherson replaced Roberge, and he came from a university. Then came Sydney Newman, James Domville, Francois Macerola, Joan Pennyfather, and now Sandra Macdonald, all managers, bureaucrats. Grierson not only loved film, he had the ear of the prime minister. That's not the case any more.

G.W. Another important filmmaker from the golden age of the NFB is Roman Kroitor, who began his filmmaking career here in Manitoba and worked with you on the local IMAX production, *Heartland* [1989]. What kind of guy was he?

C.Y. He was just like the others. He's an unassuming character, but when you sit down to talk about movies, the knowledge that man has is fantastic. And it's not just about documentary. He went into drama and IMAX. He wants to try all the new things. Like animation on IMAX and digital computerised stuff. He was into the more technical stuff.

Heartland was mainly done to attract people to the new Winnipeg IMAX theatre. Roman would have preferred *Heartland* to be more rough-edged, but he realised that it was a film sponsored by the provincial and federal governments. He wanted to make an art film in IMAX rather than a tourist film and that was a conflict for him. He had very clear ideas of what to do and felt restricted by the travelogue-tourist approach. I think he first saw it as an art film. And as an art film it's probably not successful.

He was a very unassuming guy but he couldn't be pushed around. I remember I was chairing the advisory committee on the IMAX film, which had all the deputy ministers on it plus Roman and myself. And there was a concern about native people being represented in the film. So Roman listened very patiently to Joy Constaedt[14] go on and on to present the case for inclusion of native people. When she was done, Roman calmly looked at Joy and said: 'An IMAX film won't solve all your social problems'.

G.W. But he wasn't above making movies with a social conscience. *Paul Tomkowicz, Street Railway Switchman* (1954), his first film, has a social conscience. It's about the unacknowledged finally getting noticed.

C.Y. Another Manitoban, Kathleen Shannon, had it too, the Grierson thing about the ordinary being extraordinary. But she had a different take on things. She began 'The Working Mothers series'.[15] The concept that Studio D constantly worked with was that women should come together to express

themselves. Film was simply a vehicle for that. So if you showed a film in a church hall and fifty people came and shared this common experience, then this movie was considered a success. A commonality was achieved that made people feel like they were together. Television didn't do that. Kathleen felt that television isolated women.

She told me one time that you just have to drive through Outremont[16] to see that. There's this blue light emanating from every living room. And most of the time these are women sitting alone, isolated from each other, just watching television. And I kind of felt that there was a good deal of truth to that, but you're caught. On the one hand you want your message to reach a large audience, but on the other you want it to get to an audience in a certain kind of way.

She had very solid and straightforward ideas about how films were to be distributed. I remember when the film about pornography was first shown to me, *Not a Love Story* (1981), I thought that it should be launched in a theatre, playing up its sensational side. But Kathleen did not want it to be in theatres. She and her colleagues in Studio D saw it as a movie that you show to an audience and then lead them in a discussion. Eventually, though, in Winnipeg I was able to get it into a commercial movie theatre where it did extremely well. It reached an audience that it never would have reached.

G. W. Did you ever meet John Grierson?

C.Y. I met him once – at a time when he didn't like what was going on at the Film Board, when almost every film that came out was experimental. Part of my job was to interpret these experimental films, to march in with a film, show it and then tell people what it was all about. There was a lot of experimentation then. Grierson showed up once and he was pretty perturbed. He didn't see experimental films as part of the NFB's role, which he pretty well saw as films that mirror what's wrong with our society.

G.W. What kind of a person was he?

C.Y. He was wonderful, very grumpy. He felt that experimental films were hogwash. He didn't think it was right for a federal agency to be wasting its money on self-indulgence.

G.W. Well, wasn't he more of a market-oriented guy, always aware of distribution and promotion?

C.Y. Actually, he even used to go to film councils to announce the latest film. He'd travel across the country to do it. And he was directly involved in choosing what posters should be used for the films. He'd consult with these councils on what kind of films should be made and what kind of promotional materials were needed. He had this national network – the Truro film council and the Prince Albert council[17] and others across the country to take the pulse about what was going on. He'd go to Saskatchewan and he'd find out that there was a need for windbreaks on the prairies and all of a sudden a film got made about this that got shown everywhere. And *How to Build a Hog Self-Feeder* (1944) for Prince Edward Island. He was very practical, filling immediate needs. I don't know how much influence the filmmaker had in all that. The filmmaker back then was just a vehicle.

G.W. Do you see yourself in his tradition – since you started in marketing?

C.Y. No. I don't think Grierson was necessarily looking for a more populist kind of filmmaking. I mean, take a look at *Night Mail* (1936).[18] I think

he was more interested in making the people who were working in that postal system feel better about themselves. Now we're in an age of digital technology, etc.; and it takes such expertise in marketing now that I don't think he would have approved it. I'm more interested in a popular audience than I think he was.

G.W. Speaking of popular, has television affected the NFB much?

C.Y. The more the Film Board redirects its energies towards today's television, the more they'll find that their films will change and they'll lose their identity. Because television is television. It's anonymous. People don't notice logos. Being on TV won't necessarily give the Board a public profile. The question is: do they need a public profile? I think the Film Board does.

The conflict is when you make a documentary for a half-a-million dollars, it has to be seen by the widest possible audience. Or at least it should be shown on television so the public at least gets to see

Fig. 4. Michael Curtis, the troubled street kid adopted by a gay city councillor to form *A Kind of Family*.

what it's paying for. That's the concept. The question is whether that will give the Film Board any kind of reputation. Ironically, the most successful kinds of NFB films, if you look at them historically, have been the ones that have come out of left field: *Company of Strangers* (1991), *Kahnesatake* [1993]; they were never oriented for television.[19]

G.W. What's the difference?

C.Y. Imagine that you were a CBC television executive and I came to you with plans for a film that was 100 minutes long, about the Mohawk perspective on the situation outside Montreal. Well, before you even got to the topic, you'd get stopped. One-hundred minutes is too long. TV works in 54-minute chunks. And then the exec would have some say in how it's done. It would be fascinating to see if it ever could get done for television because it's made like some of the old NFB films where you just hang out, waiting and then finding the right sequences of events that the audience could relate to emotionally. I mean it's a very good film, but it would never get made by TV people.

G.W. What other recent NFB films would you put up there with *Kahnesatake*?

C.Y. I can't think of very many others recently. Maybe *Company of Strangers*. I was watching that again the other night and I realised that there's no one else but the Film Board that could have made that film. The television gatekeepers wouldn't know how to deal with a project like that. They'd probably think it was too weird – a documentary-style movie about a bunch of old ladies getting stranded in the woods. Private co-producers, they're not willing to take a risk on stuff like that. You'd have a hard sell getting that movie financed with the help of private producers. So if there is a role for the Film Board, it's to do films like that.

G.W. You've just finished producing a documentary on the Avro Aero. What's that all about?

C.Y. That's pretty straightforward TV stuff. It's an area I've always been interested in – how do you mix entertainment and information, who is the audience for this kind of film and how do you address that audience? You can't, for instance, provide a history of the Avro Aero and expect the 18- to 30-year-old audiences to want to watch it. You have to make a choice: is this going to be educational or is it going to be a good story that keeps people's attention?

G.W. Which film of yours comes closest to your ideal? Which ones are you most proud of?

C.Y. Actually the one I'm most proud of is *A Kind of Family*. That's the one I like the best. I just find that the issues are touching on an emotional level, and at the same time the film rocks and has an edge to it. It doesn't stand still or get preoccupied with one small facet of the total issue, and the central theme of the film is, I suppose, universal: love your kids. When I show it to audiences, it works. Even on television it had an enormous response. It had one of the largest audiences when it appeared on CBC television – 750,000. Then they played it on other channels and even internationally, and it's always done really well.

At first I thought it would just be categorised as a 'gay' film, but it went beyond that, which is really satisfying, to discussions of values and stuff like that.

G.W. Didn't you have some historic battles with the NFB hierarchy on this film?

C.Y. The top brass at the Film Board didn't like *A Kind of Family* at all. They called it yellow journalism. My boss at the time, Barbara Emo,[20] was quite upset about it. In fact, they were especially bothered by the marketing because we tried to give an edge to it so that it didn't look like a serious movie about a relationship.

They even hated the poster. It has a guy on a street corner staring out at you. The confrontation of that image sort of spooked people. The NFB now look at films almost from the point of view of social workers. If you look at things from that perspective, *A Kind of Family* won't work for you. It's not for social workers. There aren't, like, ten interviews to give you the answers to this problem. The way it was made, with the roughness left in it, offended some people. Yellow journalism was what it was called. We were also criticised for the re-enactment scenes. The scene where the kid gets angry: we had to re-stage this. We had to be careful. But we had to re-stage it to get the audience to become more involved in the story. One of the things we learned is that some real people can act really well, better than professional actors. The CBC wanted us to eliminate these scenes when we sold it to them.

G.W. I understand you had trouble with *Fat Chance* too.

C.Y. *Fat Chance* was difficult to program. People would say: 'Why would you want to make a film

Fig. 5. Controversial poster for *A Kind of Family*.

about a fat guy? He just eats too much.' Or, 'Why'd you make a film about a fat guy who couldn't lose weight?' Even though the Film Board had made a previous film about the same thing – *A Matter of Fat* [1968], there was all this opinion about stuff like, medically, he's doing the wrong thing. Immediately, for the NFB it became a medical issue: the guy's too fat; he's going to die of a heart attack. How can we get that message across? It had nothing to do with the person. We kept hearing stuff like: it needs more research.

The strength of *Fat Chance* lies in the fact that we found the right character, and then we found other characters and an ending in the process of filming. Luckily for us, Rick didn't lose the weight while we were shooting. It made for a much better film, a film about the search for self-esteem. But he has lost weight since. You wouldn't recognise him now. He's dropped over 150 pounds.

G.W. Is it still difficult for regional filmmakers – being outside the corridors of filmmaking power?

C.Y. Part of the problem for the regions is that Montreal is there and we're here, and the main instrument for communication is still the telephone. Ideas are not something that are communicated well in that medium.

G.W. You've worked in Montreal and in the regional offices. Has regionalisation been better for the NFB?

C.Y. Absolutely! Just look at the movies we've made in Manitoba. And the NFB can draw on great stories like these from all over the country. We're sitting right here with the resources ready and not just off in Montreal.

The problem is that the NFB didn't build on it. The budgets, the authority, that kind of stuff was not expanded. The program was just dumped out there, and it stayed the same all along. If it were capitalised on, the Film Board would be a much different place.

G.W. Now that you are working in the private sector, do you see the NFB in a different light?

C.Y. Even though I worked closely with the private sector on co-productions when I was at the Film Board, I can now see more clearly that the film industry has changed enormously in the last few years. I even start to wonder whether we even need an NFB today. I still think that the idea is a really good one. The NFB provides the soul of our culture

and has been doing so for almost 60 years. It just needs something new. But how do you do it? It's a difficult challenge.

What role does an institution like the NFB play in a society that's getting away from film and whose people are less concerned with social issues? The audience has changed, the technology has changed, and our whole view of culture has changed. What role does the Film Board serve? I'd hate to have to come up with an answer to that.

G.W. What is your most satisfying memory as an NFB producer?

C.Y. A woman in a movie theatre after *A Kind of Family* one day told me: 'I couldn't believe it. That was my kid.' I like that idea. That people relate in a personal way rather than to something glossy or polished.

G.W. Is this something Winnipeg filmmakers did more than [filmmakers in] other places?

C.Y. Oh, yeah. No question about it! We were more willing to try new things in both production and promotion, not satisfied with what was done, what was expected. The people here thought like this, and it rubbed off on me. They were willing to try things that had the potential to be different. And I like that. I don't like to keep doing the same old things.

G.W. Who were the best filmmakers you worked with?

C.Y. John Paskievich. He reminded me in many ways of Tom Daly. A conversation with John was always a very thoughtful thing.

I'm really interested in his new Gypsies film, shooting it on high-8 and all. It's like going back to his documentary still-photography work. The ideas he had were always intriguing. The Indians of Czechoslovakia film was like that, and *Sedna* was one of my favourites. A very subtle film about white Inuit without hitting you over the head. You could just watch it and let it work its magic on you and come to your own conclusions about it without someone hammering you with a message.

G.W. Are there any projects that you regret not finishing at the NFB?

C.Y. The one that I really, really regret is a Gail Singer film called *You Can't Beat a Woman*. We started it six years ago as a sequel to *Loved, Honoured, and Bruised* (1980) as a way of solidifying our reputation for developing projects that had to

Fig. 6. The 'Indians of Czechoslovakia' in John Paskievich's *If Only I Were an Indian.*

do with abuse. Stuff like *The Crown Prince*[21] and even parts of *Daughters of the Country*. If you look at the entire NFB output in the last little while, it's amazing how many films came out of Winnipeg that deal with that particular area. Mike Scott started it and I carried on.

You Can't Beat a Woman is a more entertaining approach to the same topic. It's a 35-millimetre feature shot on super-16 which includes everything: blue screen, special effects, everything. For me it came oddly enough from Oliver Stone's *Natural Born Killers*. When I saw *Natural Born Killers* (1994), the thing that amazed me wasn't the content but the way it was put together, combining video and film with lots of amazing effects. I thought then that there was a possibility of taking an idea like domestic abuse and turning it into something really phenomenal that the audience would *want* to watch. They'd also be struck by the vast possibilities of cinema.

It's really an ambitious project. There are a lot of technical problems still to be overcome. I mean there's stuff going on in the foreground with action in the background. Lots of tricky things like that. Most people told me not to tackle it. But I said let's see what can be done.

The concept, I really hope the Film Board follows through with it the way it was intended. It should be perceived as a theatrical feature. I wouldn't even open it in Canada. I'd open it in LA or at the film festival in Palm Springs. It's a subject that's now become very important in Hollywood.

And it's got Gail Singer directing it, an outstanding filmmaker who doesn't tackle just ordinary projects. She takes on big subjects like abortion and then she'll do something like *Wisecracks*.[22] I will miss that. That's the one. All the time that I've worked at the Film Board, that's the only film I've really wanted to do.

G.W. Do you miss working for the Film Board?

C.Y. I miss the Film Board every once in a while. The NFB is not a job; it's a state of mind. Don't get me wrong, I think there's lots of things possible in the private sector. But in Canada it's basically getting money indirectly from the government to make movies, or working at the NFB where you get money directly. Or sometimes in the private sector it's a matter of finding multiple financing sources and then having too many people to satisfy. It can be difficult. People at the Film Board complain, but they don't realise how good they have it. ♣

Acknowledgements

Illustrations: Stills and posters courtesy of Ches Yetman and The National Film Board of Canada, Prairie Regional Centre.

Notes

1. See Peter Harcourt, 'The Innocent Eye: An Aspect of the Work of the National Film Board of Canada', *Sight and Sound*, vol. 34, no.1 (Winter, 1964–65). Reprinted in Seth Feldman and Joyce Nelson, eds., *Canadian Film Reader* (Toronto: Peter Martin Associates Ltd., 1977), 67–76. See also Chapters 3 and 4 in Gary Evans, *In the National Interest: A Chronicle of the National Film Board of Canada from 1949 to 1989* (Toronto: University of Toronto Press, 1991), 49–90.

2. Quoted in Peter Morris, *The Film Companion* (Toronto: Irwin Publishing, 1984), 61. For information on The Challenge for Change program, see Patrick Watson, 'Challenge for Change' and Marie Kurchak, 'What Challenge, What Change?' both reprinted in Seth Feldman and Joyce Nelson, eds., *Canadian Film Reader* (Toronto: Peter Martin Associates Ltd., 1977), 112–127.

3. Quoted by Ronald Dick, 'Regionalisation of a Federal Cultural Institution: The Experience of the National Film Board of Canada 1965–79' in Gene Walz, ed., *Flashback: People and Institutions in Canadian Film History* (Montreal: Mediatexte Publications Inc., 1986), 107–134.

4. For a more detailed account of the early days of the Prairie Regional Office see my essay 'Manitoba Filmmaking: On the Brink', *Arts Manitoba*, vol. 2, no. 2 (Winter, 1983), 4–9.

5. Tom Daly joined the NFB in 1940 and retired in 1984. He was a brilliant editor and a legendary producer whose credits are too extensive to even summarise. An ex-newspaperman, Brittain is English Canada's most produced and most honoured director, with over three dozen films to his credit. Among the most famous are *Fields of Sacrifice* (1963), *Bethune* (1964), *Memorandum* (1966), *Dreamland* (1974), *Volcano: An Inquiry into the Life and Death of Malcolm Lowry* (1976), *The Champions* (1978), and *Canada's Sweetheart* (1986). See *Donald Brittain: Never the Ordinary Way* (Winnipeg: The NFB, 1991). For a full account of Tom Daly's work see D.B. Jones, *The Best Butler in*

the Business: Tom Daly and the National Film Board of Canada (Toronto: University of Toronto Press, 1996).

6. Parts of the hour-long nightly news program on the government-funded national television network.

7. The Unit System of organising labour and assigning films was replaced by the Studio System in 1964. Studio C was responsible for documentary films.

8. *Lonely Boy* offers a bemused look at popular singer and Ottawa-native Paul Anka and the phenomenon of teenage hero-worship.

9. Fuller was an architect and social planner, famous for his geodesic domes. Wiseman and the Maysles brothers are major American documentary filmmakers, whose most influential works were done in the 1960s.

10. Guy Glover was a producer who began at the NFB in 1939 as an animator. His films, like Norman McLaren's, were camera-less and hand-drawn. In 1961 he made a compilation film *Self-Portrait*, with scenes from memorable NFB movies from 1939 to 1960.

11. Michael Rubbo, an Australian by birth, joined the NFB in 1970. His major works are *Sad Song of Yellow Skin* (1970), *Wet Earth and Warm People* (1971), *Waiting for Fidel* (1974), *Solzhenitsyn's Children* (1978), and *Daisy: The Story of a Facelift* (1983).

12. A gifted editor who contributed to many television documentaries, Don Haig has worked as a producer in the public and private sectors, for CBC and the NFB since the mid-1970s.

13. After 1965, Derek May made art and arty films, among them *Angel* (1966), *A Film for Max* (1970), *Sananguagat* (1974), *Mother Tongue* (1979) and *Off the Wall* (1981). Raxlen made impressionistic films such as *The Sky is Blue* (1969) and *Legend* (1970). Spry is best known for his political films *Flowers on a One Way Street* (1967), *Prologue* (1969), *Action* (1970) and *Reaction* (1973). He has since gone on to fiction filmmaking.

14. Joy Constaedt was an assistant deputy minister for culture in the Manitoba government at the time.

15. 'The Working Mothers' series was developed by Studio D – The Women's Studio – in 1974–75 from the *Challenge for Change* program. Eleven films of 7 to 15 minutes were eventually produced.

16. Outremont is an upper middle-class section of Montreal.

17. For an anecdotal look at Film Societies or Councils see James Beveridge, 'Grierson and Distribution' in *John Grierson and the NFB* (Toronto: ECW Press, 1984), 29–41. Truro is in Nova Scotia; Prince Albert is in Saskatchewan.

18. *Night Mail* was directed by Harry Watt and Basil Wright for Grierson's film unit at the Empire Marketing Board in England – before he came to Canada.

19. *Company of Strangers*, directed by Cynthia Scott, is the story of seven old women who become isolated in a remote cottage when their bus breaks down. It is one of the best examples of work for the NFB's Alternative Drama Program, which used amateur actors and improvised stories to examine current social issues. *Kahnesatake*, directed by Alanis Obamsawin, provides an inside look at the crisis on a native reserve south of Montreal.

20. Barbara Emo at this time was Director General of Production at the NFB.

21. *Crown Prince* (1989), directed by Aaron Kim Johnston, is a short drama which examines family abuse from the point of view of a young teenage boy.

22. Gail Singer is a versatile and socially committed filmmaker who directed the drama *True Confections* (1990) and several documentaries – including *Loved, Honoured and Bruised* (1980), the controversial *Abortion: Stories from North and South* (1984), and *Wisecracks* (1992), a performance documentary on female stand-up comics.

Film History, Volume 9, pp. 149–167, 1997. Copyright © John Libbey & Company
ISSN: 0892-2160. Printed in Australia

Historicising the 'Voice of God': The place of vocal narration in classical documentary

Charles Wolfe

n critical and historical accounts of documentary film practice, voice-over commentary in the 'classical' documentary of the 1930s and 1940s is commonly equated with a 'Voice of God'. Disembodied, this voice is construed as fundamentally unrepresentable in human form, connoting a position of absolute mastery and knowledge outside the spatial and temporal boundaries of the social world the film depicts. Vocal commentary for *The March of Time* often serves as the prototype: stentorian, aggressive, assuming a power to speak the truth of the filmic text, to hold captive through verbal caption what the spectator sees. In the 1950s and 1960s, most histories tell us, the technique was rejected as authoritarian, didactic, or reductive by filmmakers who, committed to new strategies of observation (direct cinema, cinéma vérité, cinéma direct), opted for location sound, the authenticity of which was presumably commensurate with that of the photographic image. To the extent that vocal narration remains in use – by filmmakers schooled in the *vérité* critique but seeking to recover some of the power of the voice to narrate or explain – voice-over typically is considered less assertive or homogenous than in documentaries of an earlier era: voices are personal or casual, multiple or split, fragmentary or self-interrogating, lacking a full knowledge of events or the motives and causal logic that a classical documentary would claim to disclose. [1]

The remarks to follow query standard accounts of the history of documentary voice-over from two perspectives: first, by exploring some general issues suggested by the language we currently use to describe a commentating voice in documentary; second, by considering the range of vocal strategies found in American documentaries in the early years of sound, with particular attention to *The Spanish Earth* (Ivens, 1937) and *The Battle of Midway* (Ford, 1942). If the notion of a 'Voice of God' – accepted, rejected, or deflected and dispersed – plays a central role in the way the history of documentary has come to be written, this concept also may mask those elements of sound film practice in the 1930s and 1940s that are most intriguing and instructive – instructive for what they tell us about both changing conceptions of documentary style and a field of

Charles Wolfe is associate professor and chair of the Department of Film Studies at the University of California, Santa Barbara, and has published widely on documentary films of the 1930s and 1940s. Correspondence: Department of Film Studies, University of California, Santa Barbara, CA 93106, USA.

historical cross-references that to the modern viewer may be lost.

Voice-over as metaphor

A key term in our contemporary critical vocabulary, 'voice-over' designates a *place* for vocal commentary by way of a metaphor that is at once spatial and hierarchical: voices are heard *over* ... what? Over images, we may be tempted to say, but I think this is only partially right. As the felt need for a distinction between voice-*over* and voice-*off* makes plain, at issue here is not simply synchronisation (whether vocal utterances are matched to moving lips on the screen), nor a particular sensory dimension (audition versus vision), but rather our interpretation of the relationship of voices that we hear to a world that a documentary takes as its object of regard.[2] The source of a voice heard 'off', while not visible within a given shot, is assumed to originate within a proximate visible field – off frame but from a space contiguous to and a time continuous with the depicted action. In contrast, voice-over comes from *else*where (the question of *where* else, I will take up shortly) and may entail the hierarchical relation of a voice to other sounds as well. Those who speak in voice-over may know, comment on, or drown out sounds from the world a film depicts, but the relationship is asymmetrical: voices from that register have no reciprocal power to introduce or comment on the voices that overlay this world. We might want to say, then, that voice-over covers the world of the 'diegesis' – a term as appropriate to an analysis of narrative documentaries as to narrative fictions. While the power of documentary cinema may depend in large measure on our faith in the particular recording capacities of camera and microphone, our comprehension of a 'talking' documentary film, and of those claims it makes on our attention, requires that we locate what we hear in relation to a postulated world. In short, the idea of 'voice-over' depends upon our sense of the film as a text, capable of being partitioned in ways that are conceptual or structural, not simply technological or material.

In the compound term 'voice-over', the spatial and hierarchical implications of the preposition 'over' also are joined to a word which itself connotes a certain measure of power. In common usage, 'voice' refers not simply to the physical phenomenon of a vocal utterance – the sound produced by lungs and larynx – but to the very capacity to speak, to give formal and open expression to an idea, emotion, wish, choice, or opinion. Furthermore, 'voice' may refer to the governing perspective of a text, a source or founding impulse responsible for the organisation of its surface features. This is the sense of the term, for example, employed by Bill Nichols and Jeffrey Youdelman in separate essays on voice in documentary, published in the early 1980s, in which each argues that the abandonment of the tradition of voice-over commentary by *vérité* filmmakers in the 1960s resulted in a loss of 'voice' in a larger, figurative sense.[3] Here voice is conceived, in Nichols' apt formulation, as 'that which conveys a text's social point of view', unrestricted to 'any one single code or feature, such as dialogue or spoken commentary. Voice is perhaps akin to that intangible, moiré-like pattern formed by the interaction of all a film's codes.'[4] In this fashion, the optical metaphor of 'point of view' – central to contemporary theoretical and critical writing on cinema fiction – is subsumed by one that is vocal, an appropriate choice perhaps for a genre in which a rhetorical function has often been stressed. This chain of connotations makes imaginable an acoustic equivalent to what Edward Branigan (elaborating on the optical metaphor) has labelled a text's 'point of overview' – perhaps an 'over-voice' – discernible as we ascend various 'levels' of narration to the uppermost limit of authority in a given work.[5] Or, to put this another way, we might say that voice provides a master trope for theorising the founding principles of documentary narration and rhetoric, governing the formal construction of a work of non-fiction across different stylistic registers.[6]

But I find my metaphors mixing. Can 'voice-over' seem to function as the keystone or foundation of a documentary text, *anchoring* its construction, and at the same time hover over the world upon which it comments, *covering* it like canopy? Here our attention is drawn to the fact that, as a spatial metaphor, 'voice-over' tells us nothing about the source of the voice we hear, orienting us only in terms of a negation: voice not from the image, nor from that surrounding diegetic space that images and sounds imply.[7] Where then from? Many possibilities can be cued by a film, ranging from 'places in time' subsequent to the events depicted (as with voice-over by a character, recalling an earlier event) to an extradiegetic register devoid of precise spatial or temporal definition. Pascal Bonitzer has proposed that it is precisely the lack of specificity to the origin of a vocal commentary in documentary – its nonreferential aspect – that is central to its power. From an undetermined place, evading scrutiny or critique, the disembodied voice disposes of the image.[8] From this assessment it is perhaps only a small step to the notion of a disembodied 'voice of God'. A more richly figurative label than 'voice-over', 'voice of God' also may seem to resolve the ambiguous implications of a voice at once over and under, hovering and anchoring. Omniscient, omni-present (that is to say everywhere and nowhere in particular), God may be thought of as both celestial (watching down on us) and terrestrial (inhabiting the world in all its details). The authority to describe, narrate, or interpret a world already known is thus attributed to a transcendent force.

No one, I assume, takes the 'voice of God' metaphor literally. My question is: do we even take it seriously? Whose voice would be like the voice of God? That of Cecil B. DeMille? Orson Welles? Charlton Heston?[9] Suggestions of this kind, provoked by our familiarity with roles played by these highly public personalities on and off the screen, typically are treated as jokes. Signalling the bald aspiration of the male *basso profundo* – pompous, overbearing – the term 'voice of God' carries with it an element of ridicule. Perhaps this is why it is commonly capitalised, in mock aggrandisement, pricking its pretense to authority, or is placed in quotation marks, as if culturally suspect, not to be taken at face value. At the very least, this element of pretense cues us to treat such aspirations as a fiction, a playing with God-like powers.[10]

The impulse of *verité* critics to reject vocal commentary in documentary as not simply authoritative but authoritarian, and hence to resist it, carries with it the assumption that voices layered over recorded images and sounds are in some sense detachable from the authentic filmic document. Prejudice against the immoderate ambitions of an 'over-voice' thus may betray a more fundamental, un-spoken faith in the authenticity of 'unnarrated' image and sounds, repositories of a truth that can be discerned without the interruptions or inter-ference of an invisible interpreter.[11] Amplified in motion picture theatre, imposing comment not sim-ply over the images but upon the unreceptive and immobile viewer, such a voice may convince us all the more strongly of the artifice behind its claim to mastery. The truly insidious voice, Bonitzer provo-catively suggests, is the one that does not say much; without affectation or inflection, it whispers in our ear: 'It is a layer protecting the film's image, lubri-cating it, not forcing it'.[12] In contrast, the passionate voice, or differentiated voice, at least partially re-stores a body to the voice; its contours and place of origin are imaginable. Identifiable, it encourages response and may be easier to resist.

Non-fiction talkies

Rarely do early sound documentaries from the 1930s and 1940s feature voices that whisper in our ears, and we may be inclined to resist more than a few. Yet to characterise these voices collectively as God-like is to efface the spectrum of vocal strategies employed during this period and the range of social implications these voices generated. Many of the most celebrated documentary film-makers of the period – Pare Lorentz, Willard Van Dyke, and Ben Maddow in the United States; John Grierson, Alberto Cavalcanti, Paul Rotha, and Humphrey Jennings in Great Britain – viewed the vocalisation of the non-fiction film as an opportunity for experimentation.[13] The very technological diffi-culties of recording lip-synchronised location sound prompted exploration of varied ways to match voices to documentary pictures. In an era of highly focused concern for the social dimension of the arts, close collaboration among filmmakers, writers, composers, and actors often centred on spoken narration as a key ingredient of a new kind of audio-visual work – not simply a routine travelogue or instructional film, but a vocalised 'documentary'.

In recent years, these collaborative undertak-ings have attracted renewed attention, as film his-torians have sought to reconstruct the circumstances of production in which self-consciously artful social documentary filmmaking occurred in the 1930s and 1940s.[14] Less well known, but of considerable importance to the topic at hand, are the earliest efforts of non-fiction filmmakers to adapt the technology of 'talkies' to the established format of silent travelogues and compilation films. Although many of these films do not survive, or have yet to be unearthed, press coverage of travelogues, newsreels, and films of diverse political persuasion in the 1930s hint at a wider field of activity in need of charting.[15] At the very least, reviews in *Variety* and the *New York Times*, if often sketchy, provide a sense of how the spoken word was assimilated into conventional ways of describing and evaluating non-fiction films.

Searching for a new vocabulary, reviewers tried out a wide range of labels for what we now routinely call 'voice-over': 'canned monolog', 'running monolog', 'running comment', 'synchronised dialogue', 'descriptive talks'.[16] By the mid-1930s, however, the preferred terms were 'commentary' or 'narration'. Moreover, reviewers tend to describe the voice as occurring not 'over' the depicted action but 'off-screen' or even 'off-stage' – adjectives used not in the contemporary sense of 'voice-off', but rather to designate a place for the voice external to events on the screen. Thus the *Variety* reviewer of a 1935 documentary on the search for a Jewish homeland, *Land of Promise*, praises commentator David Ross for giving the film 'a corking finishing touch with his splendid, sympathetic off-screen narration.'[17] Less happy with the results, the reviewer of *Taming the Jungle* (Paul D. Wyman, 1933) observes: 'Now and then an off-stage voice makes some comment, which is no help whatever'.[18] During the first years of talkies, in particular, terms such as 'off-screen monologue', 'off-stage lecture', and 'off-screen interlocutor' also frequently were employed.[19]

Subdued or restrained voices also tend to earn higher marks than those that are pompous, imperious or overwrought. Frank S. Nugent faulted the World War I compilation documentary, *Hell's Holiday* (1933), for having 'stridently nationalistic' commentary; a *Variety* reviewer accused the same film of mistaking 'hysterics for histrionics in the lecture'.[20] In contrast, the 'off-screen narrative' of *Lest We Forget*, produced by the Canadian Legion and released by Columbia Pictures in 1935, was praised in the pages of *Variety* for 'simple language' of a kind that neither tried to 'show for effect' nor 'gloss over the gruesomeness of war'.[21] If vocal commentary sounded implausible or otherwise ill-

suited for the images, critics also took note. 'They tell you that this group of furred people half buried in the snow of a blizzard are facing death', noted a reviewer of *Igloo*, an Arctic Circle travelogue by Ewing Scott, released by Universal in 1932. 'But the plump and cheerful looking natives don't look it. It's a case where the bare actuality, unsupported by artistic and literary trickery, doesn't register.'[22] Likewise *Gow*, E. A. Salisbury's South Seas chronicle produced the following year, was criticised for 'dialog buildup that attempts to give [the film] punch the photographed matter lacks'.[23]

Evident here is an effort to talk about the new acoustic experience of synchronised sound by way of an older tradition of the illustrated lecture, a tradition out of which the popular genre of the travelogue talkie directly emerged. Labels such as 'off-stage lecturer' or 'off-screen interlocutor' evoke the pre-talkie slide and motion picture lecture circuit, with silent pictures accompanied by a commentator purported to be familiar with the topic at hand. The voice of this lecturer had a visible place of origin: at the lectern or podium, likely to the side of the pictures. With early talkies, the absence of this lecturer may have further diminished, rather than enhanced, the authority of the voice, especially if the commentary seemed gratuitously, or otherwise inadequately, tacked on.[24] In contrast to the contemporary term 'voice-over', references to an 'off-screen' voice emphasised origin over destination, signalling more strongly the sense of a voice from a place apart.

The vocal style of *The March of Time*, in contrast, was modelled after radio drama, including the radio series of the same title launched by *Time* magazine in March 1931. As Catherine L. Covert has demonstrated, cultural discourse on radio reception in the 1920s often featured analogies between the wireless transmission of voices and supernatural forces.[25] Part of the cultural work of radio during its early commercial development was the rerouting of the fascination of listeners with the seemingly magical quality of radio transmission toward an attraction to radio personalities, familiar voices heard regularly 'on the air'.[26] Amid these developments, *The March of Time* carved out programming space for a unique kind of dramatic newscasting featuring professional actors (many of whom would go on to careers in motion pictures)

Fig. 1. Dramatic newscasting: Westbrook Van Voorhis as 'The Voice of Time'.

re-enacting events of topical interest. Narrating the series was 'The Voice of Time', a role initially performed on radio by Ted Husing and Harry Von Zell. With the commencement of a screen version under the direction of Louis de Rochemont in 1935, Westbrook Van Voorhis assumed the narrator's role, quickly mastering the eccentric ('*Time*speak') syntax, odd inflections, teletype cadence and often ironic tone that the part required. Soon a celebrity in his own right, Van Voorhis travelled and lectured extensively as a company spokesperson. As the Voice of Time, he also frequently was parodied, most famously perhaps by William Alland in the 'News on the March' segment of *Citizen Kane* (Welles, 1941).[27] Offering an arch variant on the portentous reporting of Lowell Thomas, Graham MacNee, and other radio personalities turned newsreel commentators, Van Voorhis's voice came

to represent a limit case for the theatrical embellishment of news narration on the motion picture screen.[28]

No less important a legacy than the Voice of Time, however, was the original radio program's emphasis on the distribution of speaking parts among a group of professional performers, some of whom were capable of impersonating the voices of leading figures in the news. Non-fictional radio drama, like fictional programs, entailed the orchestration of an ensemble of disembodied but easily characterised voices, the success of which was as much a matter of casting as writing. To the extent that documentary filmmakers in the 1930s and 1940s felt compelled to experiment with various mixes of vocal narration, music, and sound effects, studio broadcasting provided a workshop for exploring new ideas. The 'airwaves', in effect, came

Fig. 2. Travelogue talkies: *Eyes on Russia,* with first-person commentary by Bourke-White.

to function as an imaginary social space for vocal commentaries and the cultivating of personalities across radio and talking films.

Two distinct vocal traditions, then, can be observed here. Early travelogue talkies, ranging from the low-budget jungle films of Martin and Osa Johnson (*Congorilla* [1932], *Baboona* [1935], *Borneo* [1937]) and Frank Buck (*Bring 'Em Back Alive* [1932], *Adventure Girl* [1934]) to photo-journalist Margaret Bourke-White's politically slanted *Eyes on Russia* (1934), drew heavily on the lecturer format. By including Bourke-White, Buck, or the Johnsons within a documentary diegesis, these films linked off-screen, first-person commentaries to figures traversing exotic locales. More dramatic effects were achieved, however, through strategies of vocal re-enactment, with roots in radio drama. In social documentary films, a single narrator might speak for voiceless figures (*The Land* [Flaherty, 1941]); or interpolated voices express the thoughts or feelings of characters (*People of the Cumberland*

[Meyers and Leyda, 1938], *Valley Town* [Van Dyke, 1940]); or dialogue be exchanged across different levels of narration (*A Place to Live* [Lerner, 1940], *Fight for Life* [Lorentz, 1940]). Radio drama also seems central to the effort to soften, poeticise, or diffuse narration, as with Lorentz's integration of cadenced commentary with Virgil Thomson's folk-styled score in *The Plow That Broke the Plains* (1936) and *The River* (1937); or Stephen Vincent Benét's folk-verse commentary, read by radio actor (and *March of Time* veteran) William P. Adams, in *Power of the Land* (Ivens, 1940); or the dividing of commentary between actor Walter Huston and a less polished Anthony Veiller throughout Capra's *Why We Fight* series; or among a quartet of voices – two narrators and two soldiers, two British and two American – in the Anglo-American co-production *Tunisian Victory* (Capra and Hugh Stewart, 1944).

Sometimes awkward or stagy, devices of this kind nevertheless point to a recurring interest in finding ways to speak across and bind the separate spaces of (1) a documentary diegesis, (2) the motion picture theatre, and (3) an indefinite, mutable, and potentially fictional realm of vocal commentary that a post-synchronised soundtrack established in between. Into this last space, a variety of voices are cast. In part, vocal commentaries develop a zone of interiority, of character subjectivity, after the fashion of narrative fictions but in support of a documentary plot. But the echo of external voices in this 'off-screen' zone also may open up the film to other narratives and other social worlds.

Casting voices: *The Spanish Earth* and *The Battle of Midway*

Consider, for example, the strategic use of vocal commentary in two of the most celebrated documentaries of the period, *The Spanish Earth* and *The Battle of Midway*. The production histories of the films bear some resemblance. Shot under battlefront conditions by a crew of partisan filmmakers, both works assumed their final shape in the editing room as rare combat footage was integrated with more carefully composed images and post-synchronised sound effects, music and vocal commentary. Both films target an audience at a distance from the scene of conflict and seek to stir sentiments on behalf of a combined civilian–military campaign. Of considerable topical interest, both films were screened for Franklin and Eleanor Roosevelt in the White House, then found wider American distribution and attracted notice in the press. Although restricted in the main to art film houses and an expanding left-labour exhibition circuit, *The Spanish Earth* raised medical relief funds to aid the Spanish Republican cause, and helped to forge an alliance of anti-fascist, popular front groups in the United States prior to the onset of World War II. Distributed nationally by Twentieth Century-Fox, *The Battle of Midway* was a stimulus to a billion-dollar bond drive by Hollywood's War Activities Committee in September 1942.[29] In short, both were successful films of persuasion, made under difficult conditions to achieve concrete political goals. The patterning of vocal commentary in the two films, however, differs in ways that help to illustrate the kinds of connections and the spectrum of associations an alert spectator of documentaries could be expected to make.

Written and spoken by Ernest Hemingway, vocal narration in *The Spanish Earth* serves several conventional functions. Hemingway identifies key locations (the village of Fuenteduena, Valencia, the Tago River, the city of Madrid) and historical personages (Enrique Lister, José Diaz, Gustav Regler, La Passionária). Shifting tenses freely, he shuttles back and forth in time, most poignantly perhaps when, after identifying a former civilian lawyer and now 'brave and skillful' rebel commander, Martínez de Aragón, Hemingway reports that the officer later died during the attack on Casa del Campo. He provides sensory information the camera cannot register, as when he observes, over a long shot of a Madrid street under aerial attack, that the 'smell of death is acrid high explosive smoke and blasted granite'. He explains military tactics ('Madrid by its position is a natural fortress and each day the people make its defence more and more impregnable'), translates politically coded gestures ('the clenched fist of Republican Spain'), and underscores the structural link the film works steadfastly to draw between an irrigation project in the country and the battle for Madrid. Knowledgeable through out, he helps to orient the viewer, to clarify narrative conflicts, and to interpret the significance of events that are depicted and juxtaposed visually.

Hemingway also employs several novelistic devices that serve to psychologise the action. We are given access to the motives of a young rebel soldier, 'Julian', whose journey home to see his family in Fuenteduena strengthens the link between city and country, military service and farming. Footage of an evacuation, deftly edited by Helen Van Dongen, gains emotional power as Hemingway assumes the voice of an aging woman who is imagined to ask, 'But where will we go? ... Where can we live? ... What can we do for a living?', then another who is imagined to reply, 'I won't go. I'm too old'. More elaborate still is a leave-taking sequence, in which a contingent of soldiers depart for war. A soldier and a woman sit on a running board, with a small child standing on one side and an uninvolved soldier on the other. The narrator observes:

> They say the old-goodbyes that sound the same in any language. She says she'll wait. [Cut to another soldier and two women, one looking toward him and the other away.] He says that

Fig. 3. Ernest Hemingway's commentary for *The Spanish Earth*: 'They say the old goodbyes that sound the same in any language. She says she'll wait ...'

Fig. 6. '... Nobody knows if he'll come back. Take care of the kid, he says. I will ...'

Fig. 4. '... He says that he'll come back. He knows she'll wait ...'

Fig. 7. '... she says but knows she can't. They both know that when they move you out in trucks, it's to a battle.'

Fig. 5. '... Who knows for what, the way the shelling is ...'

he'll come back. He knows she'll wait. [Cut to a soldier standing beside a woman and four small boys.] Who knows for what, the way the shelling is. [Cut to a woman holding an infant, framed by two soldiers, one who looks toward the camera.] Nobody knows if he'll come back. [The soldier turns toward the woman, blocking her from camera view.] Take care of the kid, he says. I will. . .[cut to a military truck, as a group of women pass by in the foreground]. . .she says but knows she can't. They both know that when they move you out in trucks, it's to a battle.

With great economy, the commentary captures an interior tension between thought and speech, between what is promised or asserted and what is known to be true. Differently configured, each grouping is attended to separately by the camera, whose presence at this inescapably public moment is acknowledged by a glance. Based on the small, distinctive gestures of these men and women, it is possible to conjecture that each family has a different story to tell. At the same time the pressures and protocols of wartime parting – which inevitably leave complex feelings unexpressed – is evoked as a common, shared experience. Like the Spanish choral music we hear over the prologue, during Julian's travels home, and at the very end, Hemingway's commentary foregrounds collective emotions and patterns of thought.

Do we construe this voice as the 'voice of God'? Hemingway's authority is never called into question. He is not restricted to a single location and he moves back and forth in time. He has the power to narrate and explain events and speak for silent figures on the screen. Yet as Tom Waugh has noted in a richly suggestive dis-

Fig. 8. The 1937 playbill cover for *The Spanish Earth*.

cussion of *The Spanish Earth*, Hemingway's commentary is much closer to the tradition of documentary experiments in the 1930s and 1940s than a conventional newsreel style.[30] To begin with, Hemingway's voice does not seem to descend from on high. In part this is because of the forms of address he adopts, as when, for example, he responds acidly to a close-up of the identification plate of a downed plane, 'I can't read German either', implicitly aligning himself with the American spectator while linking the Spanish Fascists to an emergent Axis threat. At times he places himself among the villagers and foot soldiers, and invites the viewer to do so also, executing subtle shifts between the third and first persons. 'This is the moment that all the rest

of war prepares for', he notes in the closing section, 'when six men go forward into death to walk across a stretch of land and by *their* presence on it prove – this earth is *ours*'(my emphases). Reduced in number, the soldiers dig in to protect the irrigation project along the road from Valencia to Madrid. 'The bridge is ours. The road is saved,' the narrator tells us, an assertion of collective triumph that can be shared by supporters of the Republican cause around the globe.

Hemingway's voice also is never thunderous or overbearing. His spoken commentary, akin to his distinctive prose style, is concise and restrained. For long stretches, the narrator falls silent, yielding to Spanish folk songs (reworked in the style of Virgil

Thomson's regional Americana and Marc Blitz-stein's brasher, sometimes dissonant scoring); the fabricated sounds of gunfire, aeroplanes, sirens, and shattering glass (under the direction of effects editor Irving Reis of the CBS radio workshop); the speeches of leaders (some translated, some not) and anxious cries of warning or anguish ('¡Ava-ción!', called out five times, by voices of different volume, timbre and pitch).[31] Sometimes the very silence of the soundtrack is unnerving, as when victims of a bombing raid scurry down city streets, in anticipation of another explosion, the sound of which we too await. This sequence seems the inspiration for the playbill cover for the American premiere of *The Spanish Earth* at the 55th Street Playhouse in August 1937, which featured an abstract rendering of a woman and child, the mouths of both open in wide black circles, beneath the outline of three soaring airplanes. At the bottom of the page, under the title of the film, Hemingway is credited with the 'commentary and narration'. This cover artwork neatly captures the reciprocal relation between Hemingway's literate commentary, supportive but understated, and the pictorial representation of war-time anguish, for which there are no words.[32]

For many commentators in the 1930s, moreover, the casting of Hemingway as reader of his own scripted commentary reinforced the authenticity of his remarks. A rather different effect reportedly was achieved with an earlier recording of the commentary by Orson Welles, recruited by the film's sponsors in an effort to capitalise on the celebrity status of this *wunderkind* of the Federal Theatre Project and rising radio star of Archibald MacLeish's radio verse plays *Panic* (1934) and *The Fall of the City* (directed by Reis in 1937) and *The March of Time* and *The Shadow* radio series. Although this version of *The Spanish Earth* was shown at the White House and at various benefit screenings in Los Angeles, Ivens discarded it prior to *The Spanish Earth*'s general release. Its weakness, the filmmakers agreed, was largely one of tone. Van Dongen later recalled that Welles' narration was like the 'voice of God', demanding all the attention, clashing with the picture. As far as I was concerned it wrecked the film.[33] Persuaded by Van Dongen and others, Ivens opted to let the author read his own script. Hemingway's 'lack of a professional

commentator's smoothness', Ivens later remembered, 'helped you believe intensely in the experience on the screen'.[34]

Above and beyond the differing qualities to their voices, Welles and Hemingway also brought different personae to their casting in the film. Welles was a brilliant young showman, Hemingway an established man of letters. Well known in literary circles for his fascination with Spain, as evident in works of fiction (*The Sun Also Rises*, 1926; 'A Clean, Well-Lighted Place', 1933) and non-fiction (*Death in the Afternoon*, 1932), Hemingway had spent much time in that country.[35] Prior to working on *The Spanish Earth*, he assisted writers Prudencio de Pereda, John Dos Passos and Archibald MacLeish in composing the commentary for *Spain in Flames*, a tendentious (and heavily censored) documentary edited by Van Dongen from newsreel footage of the Spanish Civil War. His eyewitness reporting of the Spanish conflict, while travelling with Ivens, also appeared in the *New Republic* and via dispatches for the North American Newspaper Alliance in the months prior to and during the release of *The Spanish Earth*. In this sense, Hemingway's vocal performance was in the tradition of the informed, well-travelled, credentialled lecturer. His commentary, in Ivens' judgement, was akin to that of 'a sensitive reporter who had been on the spot and wants to tell you about it – a feeling that no other voice could communicate'.[36] While reviewers in 1937 were not of one mind in assessing the commentary's effectiveness – some found it insufficiently flamboyant or bipartisan – most reviewers paid close attention to Hemingway's vocal style, many detecting in it an echo of his terse, poetically understated and, at times, caustic prose.[37]

Vocal commentary in *The Battle Midway* functions rather differently. Ford, who had been wounded while filming the battle with his Office of Strategic Services Field Photo Unit, provided preliminary ideas for a script, but solicited successive drafts from two former collaborators, screenwriter Dudley Nichols and MGM executive James Kevin McGuinness. Working like a radio director, Ford then assigned parts from the script to four actors – Donald Crisp, Irving Pichel, Jane Darwell, and Henry Fonda – and coached them in their reading of individual lines.[38] Each of the quartet has a distinct vocal personality. Crisp's voice tends to be lilting and a bit urgent, and is most closely aligned with aerial missions. Pichel's is more formal and solemn, and he often comments on the aftermath of combat from a perspective on the ground. At the same time, both function as conventional narrators, defining settings, placing events in a temporal sequence, and attributing thoughts or emotions to individual figures (including, with laboured irony, the 'anxious' birds of Midway Island) as they are depicted on the screen.[39] The temporal mobility of Crisp and Pichel is suggested by their use of the historical present (as when Pichel intones: 'An historic council of war is held'), or by adroit shifts in tense, as when Crisp's assertion, 'Meanwhile our ships stopped the Jap fleet', is followed by the excited announcement, 'Suddenly the trap is sprung!'. Much more explicitly than does Hemingway, Crisp and Pichel also acknowledge the geographical distance between the action described and the location of the spectator, while at the same time articulating a social relationship between these separate sectors.

Defined explicitly as battlefront and homefront, these worlds are connected by the common experience of war. 'It's *our* outpost, *your* front yard', Crisp announces as we are given our first aerial view of the islands, the scene of a once and future battle, aligning himself with the naval pilots stationed far from home. But then, after victory, he crosses the boundary he had earlier drawn, reminding us collectively that '*our* front yard is safe'. Never forced to settle on one side of the battlefront/homefront divide, Crisp and Pichel provide an overview (if not at times an over-voice) for the domestic spectator, transforming what might at first appear to be an exotic travelogue into a narrative account of heroic labours along a new global 'porch front' – the Pacific theatre of war. 'Men and women of America', Pichel announces somberly as surviving pilots return, 'here come your neighbours' sons, home from a day's work. You'll want to meet them.' Vocal commentary thus provides the opportunity for a new form of greeting across a spatial gap and temporal lag that motion pictures, viewed retrospectively, inevitably disclose.

The multiplying of speaking parts, moreover, allows Ford at once to dramatise and bridge this divide. Here the voices of Darwell (overtly maternal) and Fonda (chipper, well-mannered) play crucial roles. During their initial exchange, just prior to the first round of battle, Darwell excitedly observes that a pilot resembles her 'neighbour's boy' precisely at the moment he comes into view for the spectator, foreground left. As the camera pans over to a plane, Darwell then inquires if it is 'one of those flying fortresses'. Fonda politely replies, 'Yes, ma'am it is'. Darwell names the pilot ('Why that's Will Kinney'), identifies his hometown (Springfield, Ohio), and wonders aloud if Kinney will 'fly that great big bomber'. Again, Fonda responds with plain-spoken courtesy: 'Yes ma'am, that's his job. He's the skipper.'

From what place do these characters speak? Where does their colloquy occur? The question seems relevant in a way that it doesn't for Crisp and Pichel. First of all, Darwell and Fonda's relationship to what we are watching in the film seems more circumscribed. Neither are empowered to narrate events concerning the battle: to establish temporal, spatial or causal links, or to instruct us (even indirectly) in the historical significance of what has transpired/is transpiring. Moreover, while the commentaries of Crisp and Pichel roam freely over events, those of Darwell and Fonda are limited to two occasions: the departure of pilots from Midway Island into battle, and the return of survivors in its aftermath. Furthermore, Darwell and Fonda seem engaged in an off-screen drama; they exchange dialogue, act out roles. Indeed, a logical hypothesis might be that they are watching footage from *The Battle of Midway*, perhaps sitting before us. From this place, Darwell speaks for the watchful American mother, capable of discerning in the slightest gesture – a certain gait – a telling sign of familiarity, and hence the possibility of restoring familial bonds. In counterpoint, Fonda (a serviceman on furlough? a self-educated new recruit? a military escort for Darwell?) supplies professional information – that, say, such and such a plane is indeed a flying fortress, or that piloting the bomber is young Will Kinney's job.

Darwell's comments, however, do not simply respond to the images. Her remarks seem briefly to influence the direction the film takes. She reveals more about the Kinneys of Springfield: 'Will's Dad is an engineer, 38 years on the old Ironton railroad'; his mother, sitting and knitting, with a service star on the wall behind, is 'just like the rest of us mothers

Fig. 9. *The Battle of Midway*: Battlefront ...

in Springfield or any other American town'; his sister Patricia, chatting on the telephone, is 'about as pretty as they come'. In this fashion we are taken on a short excursion from Midway Island to Springfield where, long in advance of Pichel's invitation to meet 'our neighbours' sons', Darwell introduces homefront spectators to people 'just like themselves'. Does Darwell now function as an embedded narrator, in some sense authorising the images of the people from Springfield she describes? Do these images represent her memory of these people, triggered by her recognition of Will? Are they Fonda's images too? Or does the screen now anticipate and respond to Darwell's comments, the images slotted into place by some higher-level narrator to keep pace with the verbal information she supplies? The detachment of voices from specific bodies (but surely not from the specific connotations of gender and age) thus may occasion a curious effect, whereby recorded voices, projected from theatre speakers, circulate through surrogate spectators on their way to 'covering' a diegetic plane.

However we choose to chart the flow of voices, what transpires is a fiction – on at least two counts. First, unlike the battle fought at Midway, no referent is specified for this exchange. The placeless space of voice-over is filled temporarily by an imaginable homefront vignette from which we may take pleasure or instruction, or even umbrage, but which has no concrete relation to the events that occurred at Midway, on 4–6 June 1942. Moreover, to the extent that the voices of Darwell and Fonda are highly recognisable, their exchange calls to mind a vocal intertext of film fictions. Indeed, the most proximate referent for their conversation is surely Ford's *The Grapes of Wrath*, in which Darwell and Fonda had appeared two years before: Darwell in the Academy Award-winning role of Ma Joad, espousing a family-based notion of community in a Depression-era story of social dislocation; Fonda as her son Tom, who possesses a wider range of social knowledge and by necessity breaks with the family in pursuit of social justice, taking on the burden of a larger cause at the close. Without grounding itself in the plot of this particular fiction, the exchange

Fig. 10. ... and homefront, bridged by the voices of Jane Darwell and Henry Fonda.

between Darwell and Fonda nevertheless trades in the repository of associations that this vocal intertext supplies.[40]

A trail of associations – if more faintly felt – is evoked by the performances of Crisp and Pichel as well: Crisp in his Academy Award-winning role as the patriarch of a Welsh mining family in Ford's *How Green Was My Valley* (1941); Pichel heard (but never fully seen) as the adult narrator of the same film, whose leave-taking from the valley inaugurates the retrospective telling of the story.[41] Perhaps because Crisp and Pichel themselves never engage in a fictional exchange with one another, their voices retain an autonomy that underscores their function as documentary narrators. When the pilots return to Midway Island, Fonda follows up on remarks by Crisp and Pichel, and a fervent plea by Darwell to get the injured pilots to a hospital (uttered as if it might affect the outcome of these documented events) inspires biting commentary by Crisp on the destruction of the hospital by the Japanese. But Crisp and Pichel never themselves assume the role

of characters, never descend – so to speak – into Springfield. Amid the densely orchestrated sounds of combat once the battle has commenced, Pichel intervenes to announce, 'this really happened', as if to cordon off this segment from the previous colloquy.[42] In doing so, he aligns his own commentary with a passage that is visually coded as authentic, as shock waves are registered both by an unsteady camera and by the presentation of frame lines, as if the gate of the printer, or perhaps the projector at the site of reception, has been knocked ajar by the force of an explosion.

At work here is an inversion of the interpolation of documentary passages in Hollywood fiction of the period, of say the broadcast reporting of celebrated radio news commentator Hans Kaltenborn in *Mr Smith Goes to Washington* (Capra, 1939), who is recruited to add a trace of authenticity to the story of a senate filibuster, yet whose presence never throws the fiction off course.[43] Although *The Battle of Midway* bills itself at the outset as simply a record or report by Navy photographers, the labours of Ford, his writers, and his stock company of actors point to a rather different notion of what can count as an appropriate documentary experience. For spectators in a commercial motion picture theatre, *The Battle of Midway* traded overtly with the conventions of Hollywood fiction. Vocal commentary by Darwell and Fonda, in particular, is less a ground of authority than a tool to expand the ways in which authenticated images can be interpreted, with narrators and proto-characters interposed between the spectator and a presupposed, projected world. In this fashion, *The Battle of Midway* from fiction elements of melodrama even as it anticipates, in its memorable combat footage, the expressive immediacy of *verité*, whose practitioners rejected theatrical vocal effects.

Recasting the 'Voice of God'

Unlike reflexive, modernist, or postmodern documentaries of more recent vintage, both *The Spanish Earth* and *The Battle of Midway* secure a causal logic for the action they depict, and never call the authority of their vocal commentaries into question. But in a way that the notion of 'Voice of God' narration does not suggest, these documentaries also employ forms of verbal address and verbal tenses that define a complex spatial and temporal relation among commentator, spectator, and documented events. Moreover, the films seem keenly aware of the social qualities and distinctions that a disembodied voice can evoke and draw on familiar personalities precisely for the associations their voices provide. Conventional notions of voice-over narration notwithstanding, this should not surprise us. As Sarah Kozloff has observed with respect to the use of voice-over in classical Hollywood fiction, nothing prevents a third-person narrator, however disembodied, from revealing something about his or her world, nor the spectator from scrutinising and evaluating what this narrator has to say. Concomitantly, the grounding of a visible narrator in a particular location does not necessarily delimit the range of knowledge nor diminish the potential authority of that figure. In either case, spectators make judgements about the reliability and import of what they hear. As Kozloff notes, 'the moral and political questions concerning voice-over, do not revolve around its unique essence, but around how film-

makers use it – what they have the narrator say, and in what manner'.[44] It is the very specificity of the use of vocal narration in persuasive documentaries such as *The Spanish Earth* and *The Battle of Midway* to which we must attend.

Judgements concerning the pertinence and explanatory power of vocal narration in a documentary involve many factors, only one of which – and perhaps not always the most compelling given the sensory pleasures and motor force of motion pictures – is the logic of an argument. Above and beyond and even against matters of coherence and plausibility, we may also find vocal commentary attractive for its felicitous language, appealing verbal rhythms, or fresh expression of familiar sentiments. Interplay among a variety of voices likewise may arrest attention. Many social documentary filmmakers in the 1930s and 1940s were willing to explore and exploit these attractions, to experiment with poetic or colloquial language, diffused authority, and polyvocalism. In part, this seems inspired by a desire to produce the kind of variegated subjectivity common to classical fiction. But it may also reflect an impulse to expand the range of narrational options through the interpolation of extrinsic, ambiguously situated voices. In contrast to classical fiction, the effect often is to render fuzzy the boundaries of the non-fictional world upon which a documentary film is premised. Imported voices thus may invoke complementary worlds (including the imagined worlds of fiction) which the viewer is invited to consider in relation to the main, documented event.[45]

Faced with a potential disjunction between a documentary's referential field and the uncertain ground for disembodied voices, a spectator is encouraged to locate, and infer connections across, a variety of social markers. The invisible realm of 'voice-over' thus should itself be construed as preeminently social, an historical understanding of which demands the reconstruction of a broader vocal intertext encompassing fiction films and radio dramas. To chart such a space is not to presume that we can know the horizon of expectations of all historically situated spectators – a task itself without boundaries. Nor is it to specify the necessary effect of any particular vocal strategy – a generalisation built on quicksand. Nevertheless, accounts of reception may bring into relief associations and assump-

Fig. 11. Darwell and Fonda as Ma and Tom Joad in *The Grapes of Wrath*.

tions that have lost salience over time. Having no difficulty identifying Ford's allusion to the Joad family in *The Battle of Midway*, for example, several (male) reviewers found Darwell's dialogue in particular to be excessive and overwrought. Critic Manny Farber, seizing an opportunity to scold wartime documentary filmmakers for emphasising words at the expense of images, in a review that anticipates a *vérité* critique, ridiculed the vocal commentary in *The Battle of Midway* as 'high school dramatics', incommensurate with the compelling images of men in battle.[46] Yet the film's editor, Robert Parrish, recalls hearing women sob at the film's Radio City Music Hall premiere, an event that fulfilled Ford's ambition to open up an entry point in the story of the battle for 'the mothers of America'.[47] The fictive space Darwell and Fonda occupy, if variously judged, thus takes on definition by way of references extrinsic to the film's ostensible

subject and largely unavailable to the modern viewer.

Construing the placeless space of vocal narration in documentary as fundamentally social and historical brings to light the limits of 'voice-over' as a metaphor to describe the varied kinds of work that vocal commentary performs. It draws our attention to a field of vocal references in which the non-fiction 'talkies' of the period circulated, a lateral file of vocal possibilities from which these films drew, and brings into sharper focus the stress points in those works for which a necessary and sometimes awkward split between sound and image occasioned an experimental approach. It encourages us to explore precisely those features that are occluded by the conventional notion of 'voice of God' narration, retrospectively and uniformly applied: the historical resonances of vocal acts – how accents, inflections, and forms of speech reverberate across and double back over fiction and non-fiction, film and radio, in the media dialect and dialogue of another era. ♣

Acknowledgement

I wish to thank Edward Branigan, Nataša Durovicová, and Michael Renov for their comments on a previous version of this essay.

Notes

1. For an influential topology of modes of documentary representation based on an historical sketch of this kind, see Bill Nichols, 'The Voice of Documentary', *Film Quarterly* (Spring, 1983), 17–29, reprinted in *Movies and Methods*, vol. 2, ed., Nichols (Berkeley: University of California Press, 1985), 258–273, and revised in Nichols, *Representing Reality* (Bloomington: Indiana University Press, 1991), 32–75. Nichols takes pains, however, to stress that the four modes are not exclusive to any single historical period.

2. On the utility of the distinction between voice-off and voice-over, see Mary Ann Doane, 'The Voice in the Cinema: The Articulation of Body and Space', *Yale French Studies*, 60 (1980): 33–50, especially 37–43.

3. Nichols, 'The Voice of Documentary'; Jeffrey Youdelman, 'Narration, Invention, & History: A Documentary Dilemma', *Cineaste*, 12, no. 2 (1982): 8–12. Youdelman prefaces his remarks with a useful discussion of some prototypes from the 1930s and 1940s, including *The New Earth* (Ivens, 1934), *Night Mail* (Wright and Watt, 1936), *The River* (Lorentz, 1937), *The City* (Van Dyke and Steiner, 1939), *Native Land* (Strand and Hurwitz, 1942), and *Strange Victory* (Hurwitz, 1948).

4. Nichols, 'The Voice of Documentary', 18. In his revised discussion of the topic, Nichols chooses to replace the term 'voice' with 'argument', as carried by both 'commentary' and 'perspective'. A 'loss of voice', then is reformulated as 'a deferential perspective, one that chooses to present evidence of the world as witnesses describe it rather than add a contrapuntal argument or voice of its own' (*Representing Reality*, 281, endnote no. 17). In opting for a term unencumbered by the acoustic connotations of 'voice', Nichols thus chooses to emphasise the polemical, rather than more broadly expressive, dimension of a documentary's underlying 'social point of view'.

5. Edward Branigan, *Narrative Comprehension and Film* (London: Routledge, 1992), 115.

6. Carl Plantinga adopts just such a trope in *Rhetoric and Representation in Non-Fiction Film* (Cambridge University Press, 1997), in which he usefully outlines three broad epistemological functions for documentary, based on the degree of narrational authority, and labels these the 'classical', 'open', and 'poetic' voices of non-fiction.

7. That we can respond to sound waves, but not light waves, without knowing their source suggests the rather different ways we think about audition and vision. As Edward Branigan notes, while we tend to believe that sound waves travel to our ears, we conceive light waves as a property of an object viewed; hence, for example we imagine that the 'red' cover of a book retains its colour even in a lightless room. 'When we see a "lamp" and can name it, the identification is complete but a "whistling" sound still needs to be specified: the whistling of what? from where?' See Branigan, 'Sound and Epistemology in Film', *The Journal of Aesthetics and Art Criticism*, vol. 47, no. 4 (Fall, 1989): 311.

8. Pascal Bonitzer, 'Les Silences de la voix', *Cahiers du cinéma*, 246 (February–March 1975), translated as 'The Silences of the Voice (*A Propos* of *Mai 68* by Gudie Lawaetz)' in *Narrative, Apparatus, Ideology: A Film Theory Reader*, ed. Philip Rosen (New York: Columbia University Press, 1986), 324. Bonitzer's ideas are elaborated upon by Doane in 'The Voice in Cinema', 42; and Kaja Silverman in *The Acoustic Mirror: The Female Voice in Psychoanalysis and Cinema* (Bloomington: Indiana University Press, 1988), 48–49, 51–54, and 163–164.

9. It is interesting to note that in *The Next Voice You Hear* (Wellman, 1950), a fiction film that seeks to take seriously the question of God's vocal intervention in the lives of ordinary American citizens by way of the radio, God's voice is precisely the one that we do not hear. Instead, we learn of God's advice from characters, tuned to their radios, while the spectator through various plot devices is kept out of earshot.

10. In a work of non-fiction, what do we make of this pretence to God-like powers? Can a non-fictional world be construed as 'authored' by the same force a vocal narrator represents? Or does the non-fictional status of the image strain any claim such a narrator might make about its creative powers? Note, for example, this scripted disclaimer of authorship in the credits to *With Car and Camera Around the World*, a silent travelogue by 'Aloha and Walter Wanderwell', released in 1929: 'Author, God, for he created the earth and its people. Scenario by All Peoples' (quoted in *Motion Picture News* (21 December 1929): 40).

11. Explaining his aversion to 'Voice of God' narration,

Ricky Leacock notes: 'When I become intrigued by theatre or film or even education, it is when I am not being told the answer. I start to find out for myself ... The moment I sense that I'm being told the answer I start rejecting' (James Blue, 'One Man's Truth – An Interview with Richard Leacock', *Film Comment* (Spring, 1965): 16). Bonitzer and Doane critique the naivety of such a view. A lively defence of authoritative vocal commentary, moreover, can be found in J. Ronald Green, 'The Illustrated Lecture', *Quarterly Review of Film and Video,* vol.15, no. 2 (1994), 1–23.

12.   Bonitzer, 327.

13.   See especially Willard Van Dyke, 'The Interpretive Camera in Documentary Film', *Hollywood Quarterly,* vol. 1, no. 4 (1946): 405–409, reprinted in *Nonfiction Film Theory and Criticism,* ed. Richard Meram Barsam (New York: Dutton, 1976), 342–349; Ben Maddow, 'The Writer's Function in Documentary Film', *Writers' Congress: The Proceedings of the Conference Held in October 1943 Under the Sponsorship of the Hollywood Writers' Mobilisation and the University of California* (Berkeley: University of California Press, 1944), 98–103; Pare Lorentz, *FDR's Moviemaker: Memoirs and Scripts* (Reno: University of Nevada Press, 1992); John Grierson, 'The G.P.O. Gets Sound', *Cinema Quarterly* (Edinburgh), vol. 2, no. 4 (Summer 1934): 215–221, and 'Two Paths to Poetry', *Cinema Quarterly,* vol. 3, no. 4 (Summer, 1935): 194–196; Alberto Cavalcanti, 'Sound in Films', *Films* (November, 1939): 25–39; and Paul Rotha, *Documentary Film* (London: Faber & Faber, 1939, 2nd edn.), 201–223. Although my comments in this essay are restricted to documentary filmmaking in the United States, they are applicable to much British (or 'Griersonian') documentary from the same period.

14.   William Alexander, *American Documentary Film from 1931 to 1942* (Princeton, N.J.: Princeton University Press, 1981); Russell Campbell, *Cinema Strikes Back: Radical Filmmaking in the United States, 1930–42* (Ann Arbor, Michigan: UMI Research Press, 1982); Jonathan Buchsbaum, 'Left Political Filmmaking in the West: The Interwar Years', in *Resisting Images: Essays on Cinema and History,* ed., Robert Sklar and Charles Musser (Philadelphia: Temple University Press, 1990); Paul Arthur, 'Jargons of Authenticity (Three American Moments)', in *Theorizing Documentary,* ed., Michael Renov (New York: Routledge/AFI Film Readers, 1993), 108–134; Charles Wolfe, 'The Poetics and Politics of Nonfiction: Documentary Film', in *Grand Design: Hollywood as a Modern Business Enterprise, 1930–39,* ed., Tino Balio (New York: Charles Scribner's Sons, 1993), 351–386,

and 'Straight Shots and Twisted Plots: Social Documentary and the Avant-Garde in the 1930s', in *Lovers of Cinema: The First American Film Avant-Garde, 1919–45,* ed., Jan-Christopher Horak (Madison: University of Wisconsin Press, 1996), 234–266.

15.   For important new work in this area, see Dana Benelli's superb PhD dissertation, 'Jungles and the National Landscape: Documentary and Hollywood Cinema in the 1930s' (University of Iowa, 1992).

16.   Anon., review of *The Break Up, Variety* (6 August 1930): 35; Frank S. Nugent, review of *Hell's Holiday, New York Times* (15 July 1933): 14; 'Land'., review of *Bring 'Em Back Alive, Variety* (21 June 1932): 14; 'Char.', review of *Explorers of the World, Variety* (22 December 1931): 19.

17.   'Bige.', review of *Land of Promise, Variety* (27 November 1935): 30.

18.   'Chic.', review of *Taming the Jungle, Variety* (6 June 1933): 14.

19.   'Shan.', review of *Hei Tiki, Variety* (5 February 1935): 31; 'Rush'., review of *Igloo, Variety* (26 July 1932): 17.

20.   Nugent, 14; 'Kauf.', review of *Hell's Holiday, Variety* (18 July 1933): 37.

21.   'McStay.', review of *Lest We Forget, Variety* (17 April 1935): 15.

22.   'Rush.', review of *Igloo,* 17.

23.   'Char.', review of *Gow, Variety* (5 December 1933): 17.

24.   One reviewer, for example, complained that the Cameo Theatre in New York misleadingly promoted travelogues as entertaining, rather than strictly educational, films by advertising those with vocal accompaniment as 'all-talking' (Anon., review of *The Bottom of the World, Variety* (16 July 1930): 29).

25.   Catherine L. Covert, 'American Sensibility and the Response to Radio, 1919–24', in *Mass Media Between the Wars: Perceptions of Cultural Tensions, 1918–24,* ed. Covert (Syracuse, New York: Syracuse University Press, 1984), 199–220.

26.   Erik Barnouw, *The Golden Web: A History of Broadcasting in the United States, 1933–53* (New York: Oxford, 1968), passim; Hector Chevigny, 'Commercial Radio Writing in Wartime', *Writers' Congress,* 141–152.

27.   Raymond Fielding, *The March of Time, 1935–51* (New York: Oxford University Press, 1978), 102–110, 220–221, 260–262; Bruce Cook, 'Whatever

Happened to Westbrook Van Voorhis?', *American Film* (March 1977), 25–29.

28. Less celebrated, but notable for the pattern of migration from radio journalism to film their careers illustrate, were Malcolm La Prada, a radio travel talk narrator who provided vocal commentary for Bray Pictures' *Rambling Reporter* travel talk film series in 1930; NBC's Alois Havorille, narrator for *This is America* beginning in 1933; and NBC's Floyd Gibbons, commentator for *With Byrd at the South Pole* (1934).

29. On the production and distribution history of *The Spanish Earth*, see Joris Ivens, *The Camera and I* (New York: International Publishers, 1969), 103–138, reprinted as 'Spain and *The Spanish Earth*', in Barsam, 349–375; Thomas Waugh, 'Men Cannot Act in Front of the Camera in the Presence of Death: Joris Ivens' *The Spanish Earth*', *Cineaste*, vol. 7, no. 2 (1982): 30–33 and vol. 7, no. 3 (1983): 21–29; Thomas P. McManus, 'Down to Earth in Spain', *New York Times* (25 July 1937): x:4; and Ben Bellitt, 'The Camera Reconnoiters, *The Nation* (20 November 1937); reprinted in Lewis Jacobs, ed., *The Documentary Tradition* (New York: W. W. Norton, 2nd edn., 1979), 142. On *The Battle of Midway*, see Tag Gallagher, *John Ford: The Man and His Films* (Berkeley: University of California Press, 1986), 200–213; Robert Parrish, *Growing Up in Hollywood* (New York: Harcourt, Brace, Janovich, 1976), 144–151; 'TMP', 'Film of "Midway" Released by Navy', *New York Times* (20 September 1942): 19; Anon., '18 Minutes of Midway', *Newsweek* (21 September 1942): 80. Prior to the film's general release, *The Spanish Earth* was widely seen in Hollywood, where its audience included director John Ford (McManus, 'Down to Earth in Spain': x, 4).

30. Waugh, *Cineaste,* vol. 7, no. 3 (1983), 25–26.

31. Irving Reis devised the sound of a bombardment in *The Spanish Earth* by recording in reverse an earthquake effect from *San Francisco*, the popular fiction film released by MGM the previous year (Ivens, 129). Reis' background in radio drama paved the way for his work as a screenwriter at Paramount in 1938 and his career as a Hollywood director to follow.

32. A copy of the playbill can be found in file H139, Thomas Brandon Collection, Film Study Center, Museum of Modern Art, New York.

33. Ben Achtenberg, 'Helen Van Dongen: An Interview', *Film Quarterly* (Winter, 1976–77): 52.

34. Ivens, 128.

35. Carlos Baker, *Ernest Hemingway: A Life Story* (New York: Charles Scribner's, 1969), 299; Edward F. Stanton, *Hemingway and Spain: A Pursuit* (Seattle: University of Washington Press, 1989), 150–154; Robert O. Stephens, *Hemingway's Nonfiction: the Public Voice* (Chapel Hill: University of North Carolina Press, 1968), 88–108; Alexander, 151–152.

36. Ivens, 129. Many critics agreed: 'So simple, so real, so patently the voice of truth' (Cedric Belfrage, excerpted review, File H139, Thomas Brandon Collection); 'The beauty of simple things and felt simply said' (*London Observer*, File H139, Thomas Brandon Collection); 'Hemingway's voice – for he speaks the commentary himself – cuts through the sound of crackling battle' (Basil Wright, '*The Land Without Bread* and *The Spanish Earth*', *Film News* (December 1937), reprinted in Jacobs, 147). Alberto Cavalcanti found Hemingway's commentary the fulfillment of Wordsworth's definition of poetry: 'emotions recollected in tranquillity' (29).

37. 'JTM' [John T. McManus], 'The Screen', *New York Times* (21 August 1937): 7; John T. McManus, 'Realism Invades Gotham', *New York Times* (22 August 1937): x, 3; James Shelley Hamilton, *National Board of Review* (October 1937, reprinted in Stanley Hochman, ed., *From Quasimodo to Scarlet O'Hara: A National Board of Review Anthology* (New York: Frederick Ungar, 1982), 262–263; and reviews by 'JDH' in *New York Sun* (23 August 1937), by Gould Cassel in *The Brooklyn Daily Eagle* (24 August 1937), and anonymously in the *London Times* (9 November 1937), excerpted and collated in File H139, Thomas Brandon Collection. Hemingway's text subsequently was published in book form as *The Spanish Earth* (Cleveland: J. B. Savage Co., 1938).

38. Parrish, 146–150. Nichols previously had worked with Ford on nine features and had written the commentary for Joris Ivens' *The 400 Million* (1939), a compilation documentary made in support of China's struggle against Japan in the 1930s.

39. In a perceptive discussion of *The Battle of Midway* in *Rhetoric and Representation in Nonfiction Film*, Carl Plantinga draws a distinction between the voice of Crisp, a zealous patriot describing combat in a tendentious fashion, and that of Pichel, a gentle father or spiritual leader possessing moral authority (160). An extrapolation of character traits of this kind is interesting to consider in light of the separate contributions of writers Nichols, a political liberal, and McGuire, a conservative, and the tension between military ardour and moral authority in several of Ford's fiction films, including *Drums Along the Mohawk* (1939), *They Were Expendable* (1945), *Fort Apache* (1948), *She Wore a Yellow Ribbon* (1949), and *The Horse Soldiers* (1960). While

Ford's fiction films tend to plot this tension as narrative conflict, the voices of Crisp and Pichel serve complementary functions here.

40. Ford was identified as the director of both *The Grapes of Wrath* and *How Green Was My Valley* in the first news item on *The Battle of Midway* in *New York Times*, 'Footnotes on Headlines' (20 September 1942): 4, 2. At the time that Darwell and Fonda were recruited for vocal roles on *The Battle of Midway*, they were working together on *The Ox-Bow Incident* (Wellman, 1943) at Twentieth Century-Fox. Shortly thereafter, Fonda enlisted in the Navy and served in the Pacific. Darwell later reprised her role as Ma Joad in a radio version of *The Grapes of Wrath* on NBC's *University Theater* on New Year's Day, 1949.

41. Pichel's vocal authority similarly was exploited in *Happy Land* (1943), a wartime drama directed by Pichel, in which his voice is heard over a radio, announcing news of the outbreak of war in Europe.

42. According to Parrish, this line was initially uttered by Ford during a screening session with Nichols (147).

43. From this perspective, Kaltenborn's vocal and physical performances as noted commentator across radio and film, and fiction and non-fiction, warrant further study. Consider, for example, his casting by Orson Welles in *Julius Caesar* for a *Mercury Theater of the Air* radio broadcast in the fall of 1938, or Kaltenborn's appearance as a radio commentator, interviewing a Nazi official played by an actor, in *The March of Time* episode, 'On Foreign Newsfronts', in September 1940. Gaining great public prominence for his dramatic reports on the Munich Conference in the summer of 1938, Kaltenborn also was a CBS analyst in Spain during the Civil War (see Barnouw, 74–75). I explore the implications of Kaltenborn's appearance as a non-fictional character within the fictional context of '*Mr Smith Goes to Washington*: Democratic Forums and Representational Forms', *Close Viewings: An Anthology of New Film Criticism,* ed. Peter Lehman

(Tallahassee: Florida State University Press, 1990), 321–326.

44. Sarah Kozloff, *Invisible Storytellers: Voice-Over Narration in American Fiction Film* (Berkeley: University of California Press, 1988), 97.

45. Drawing a distinction between the tests we apply to fictional and non-fictional narration, Edward Branigan proposes that with fiction we start with 'lower' level pictures or words from which we seek to infer 'a plausible set of higher mediations with which to justify depicted events', while with non-fiction we start with beliefs in a historically real, unmediated event and the recording capacities of camera and microphone, and infer from this what 'lower' level pictures or words plausibly could be known about that event. 'Both classical fiction and classical non-fiction', he writes, 'attempt to discover meanings that lie "behind" (beyond, below) events; they merely start in different places and one expands, while the other contracts, the levels of narration' (*Narrative Comprehension and Film* (London: Routledge, 1992), 204–205.) Note the two qualifying prepositions for 'behind' suggested here. 'Beyond' (but not 'below') opens up the possibility that meanings may relate to one another not only hierachically (more or less deeply embedded in the text) but perhaps also to the side (or outside?) of the documentary diegesis.

46. 'TMP', 'Film of "Midway"', 19; Bosley Crowther, 'Citation for Excellence', *New York Times* (20 September 1942), sec. 8: 3; Sam Harold, 'Disappointed in "Midway" Film', *New York Times* (18 October 1942), sec. 8: 5; Manny Farber, 'Memorandum to Hollywood', *New Republic* (5 October 1942), 414–415. Assuming the voice of an unhappy respondent to *The Battle of Midway*, Farber speaks directly to the filmmakers: 'So plus everything else, it's a quiz show you give us: who belongs to the voice? Up till now one voice would do you. In "Midway" you have most of the Joad family, in addition to a character actor I haven't guessed yet. Donald Crisp, Henry Fonda, Jane Darwell and Mr X. A symphony of discord' (414).

Film History, Volume 9, pp. 168–188, 1997. Copyright © John Libbey & Company
ISSN: 0892-2160. Printed in Australia

The German–Russian film (mis)alliance (DERUSSA): Commerce & politics in German–Soviet cinema ties

Thomas J. Saunders

n the second half of the 1920s Soviet cinema won international acclaim through distribution and exhibition in Germany. Spearheaded cinematically by Sergei Eisenstein's *Bronenosets Potemkin* (Battleship Potemkin, 1925) and organisationally by Willi Münzenberg's Workers' International Relief and its subsidiary, Prometheus-Film, this acclaim prompted Russia's Sovkino to expand international ties by creating a joint German–Soviet company. The German–Russian Film Alliance (Deutsch-russische Film-Allianz, better known by the acronym Derussa) was founded in Berlin in late 1927 to market Soviet pictures abroad and co-produce films suitable for both the Russian and international market. Between early 1928 and mid-1929 Derussa brought a dozen Soviet features to Germany and laid the groundwork for sale of Soviet pictures to other European countries. It then collapsed in spectacular fashion, leaving in its wake a mass of debts and much ill-will. Its fortunes, historically all but ignored, represent a microcosm of the business and political di-

lemmas posed by film interchange between the Soviet Union and the West in the 1920s.

Weimar Germany and the Soviet Union have long been recognised as unlikely partners in a 'community of fate' after World War I. Both newly-founded and diplomatically isolated, they were drawn together by shared economic and strategic interests. Complementing these interests was a rich cultural interchange in which the motion picture played a noteworthy role.[1] Germany's contribution to early Soviet cinema was indispensable. As Europe's leading producer of motion pictures it sup-

Thomas Saunders is associate professor at the University of Victoria. His publications include *Hollywood in Berlin* (Berkeley: University of California Press, 1994) and articles treating national identity, war and society in German cinema. Correspondence: Department of History, Box 3045, University of Victoria, Victoria, B.C., Canada V8W 3P4. Tel. (250) 721 - 7405.

plied the bulk of the movie entertainment in Soviet theatres in the first half of the 1920s. Its prominence as a manufacturer of film stock and equipment made it the crucial source of technical apparatus. The Communist Party of Germany, the most significant outside the Soviet Union, came under the sway of the Comintern and was accessible for Soviet propaganda abroad. Through Münzenberg's Workers' International Relief (IAH) it also provided funding for Soviet production. Finally, despite reintroducing film censorship, the German Republic proved more open than the other major states of the western world to exhibition of Soviet pictures. In sum, Germany not only helped rebuild Russian cinema's shattered infrastructure but also offered crucial assistance in its breakthrough to international respectability.[2]

The Soviet contribution to Weimar cinema was likewise substantial. Apart from serving as one of Germany's largest film export markets, Russia supplied emigré performers, directors, scenarists and set designers, often employed to produce 'Russian' films in Germany. Russian settings, dramaturgy and performing styles, already stereotyped in the work of German filmmakers, acquired the air of authenticity with the arrival, in part via Paris, of these artists and producers. In addition, and most memorably, the Soviet Union provided the 'revolutionary' pictures which from 1926 gained an enthusiastic following. Young directors such as Sergei Eisenstein and Vsevolod Pudovkin offered novel and exciting paradigms for German filmmakers; in select instances their work also proved highly successful commercially. In both regards 'German film in the second half of the 1920s and until 1933 is unthinkable without the influence of Russian/Soviet cinema'.[3]

The formal ties between German and Soviet cinema most familiar to historians are those represented by Münzenberg's IAH and Prometheus-Film. The former was founded in Germany in 1921 to collect funds for famine relief in Russia. It quickly adopted film as a medium useful for disseminating awareness of Soviet Russia's dire economic situation. It also became the Soviets' principal propaganda arm in Germany as well as the conduit through which Russia acquired film stock and equipment. Münzenberg utilised IAH to help finance the credit-starved Soviet film industry. In 1924 he pro-

vided funding through IAH for the creation of a Soviet production company, Mezhrabpom-Rus, which was to provide many of the pictures that after mid-decade won international admiration. The following year he founded a German subsidiary of IAH, Prometheus-Film, which became the main source of Soviet film releases in Germany and participated with Mezhrabpom in a co-production programme.[4]

Münzenberg's IAH was central to German–Russian film ties, especially to the export of Soviet pictures, but it did not monopolise that trade. From mid-decade the Soviets distributed their films in Germany through a number of firms outside Prometheus.[5] Moreover, they responded to the international celebrity status of their young directors by launching a second major export initiative, the German–Russian Film Alliance (Derussa), which made German–Soviet cooperation its title and programme. Although ultimately short-lived, it signalled a significant extension of Soviet film ties with the capitalist West beyond the Party concerns represented by the Münzenberg organisation. Derussa's brief lifespan coincided with the transition from silent to sound film as well as fundamental upheaval in Soviet politics and culture as Stalin asserted control. Since it lacked the overt political dimension of Prometheus and drowned in a sea of recriminations and red ink two years after it was founded, it has suffered historical neglect and misrepresentation.[6] Nonetheless, as both the culmination and the last gasp of German–Soviet film collaboration before Nazification and Stalinisation, it presents an illuminating case study in the possibilities and limitations of German–Soviet cooperation at a critical juncture in film history.

Derussa's aim was to place German–Soviet film ties on a broad commercial footing like that which linked Hollywood and Berlin. It capitalised on the growing recognition of the Soviet Union in general and on the breakthrough of Soviet cinema abroad in particular. This breakthrough can be clearly dated to the release in Berlin in April 1926 of *Battleship Potemkin*. Soviet cinema became almost instantaneously a topic of international attention. In Germany an extended censorship controversy – *Potemkin* was twice banned and re-released after much lobbying from conflicting interests – helped make the picture one of the box office hits of 1926.[7] Timing proved likewise optimal. Film enthusiasts, increasingly weary of Hollywood and European imitations of Hollywood, received Eisenstein's formally novel and passionate tribute to the revolution of 1905 as a breath of cinematic fresh air. The premiere of *Potemkin* demonstrated that Soviet films could do more than address Communist party rallies or the avant-garde, and unleashed a wave of interest both in revolutionary topics and in Soviet cinematography.[8] The stylistic devices characteristic of the younger Soviet directors became the object of discussion and imitation. *Battleship Potemkin* also opened opportunities for Soviet film artists to visit the West and be lionised as cinematic pioneers. Since the Soviets' window on the West was Germany, Berlin served as the primary destination and the obvious site of an attempt to exploit export possibilities.

Derussa was the primary vehicle for tapping the commercial potential of Soviet cinema abroad. Unlike Prometheus, whose political and commercial interests overlapped with those of its Soviet partner, Derussa linked a state-owned Russian company, Sovkino, with a private, politically non-aligned German firm, Filmwerke-Staaken. Sovkino, established in late 1924, sought to concentrate the film activity of the new Russia and realise the distribution monopoly which its predecessor, Goskino, had failed to build.[9] Its commission, to create a cinema both socialist and popular, meant, on the one hand, to serve the propaganda wishes of the Party and 'cinefy' the Soviet countryside. It had, on the other hand, to support itself through distribution of imported films whose revenues would in turn yield capital for production popular enough to win back the domestic market. The breadth and official character of this assignment made Sovkino particularly susceptible to political manipulation. Despite some impressive accomplishments in its first few years, it ended up a pawn in the cultural revolution of the late 1920s.[10]

Sovkino's German partner, Filmwerke-Staaken, was effectively less a company than an entrepreneur with a checkered past, not least in links with Russia. Georg Sklarz was a wartime associate of the wealthy and flamboyant socialist Alexander Helphand (Parvus) and a participant in negotiations to spirit Lenin back to Russia in 1917. Sklarz was catapulted into notoriety during the German revolution of 1918–19 by business dealings with the new authorities, among them a venture to supply Republican troops which defended the Reichstag in the political violence of early 1919.[11] Together with one brother, Heinrich, who acted briefly during the revolution as unofficial deputy police commissioner in Berlin, and another, Jean, he came under criminal investigation for bribery, defrauding the public purse and profiteering through trade in scarce materials. Sklarz became a prominent target in postwar anti-Semitic and anti-socialist smear campaigns.[12]

In 1922–23 Sklarz ventured into the motion picture industry, acquiring a production/distribution company, Phönix-Film A.G., and financing a studio, Filmwerke-Staaken. The former was one of numerous smaller German firms; the latter, established in an airship hangar, was Europe's largest. Here Hans Neumann, one of the unsung visionaries of Weimar film production, created a monumental pageant of the life of Christ, *INRI* (1923). It was here as well that Fritz Lang shot the flood scene in *Metropolis* (1926), putting the entire 10,000 square metres of the main hall under water. Filmwerke-Staaken represented Sklarz's major asset and served as the formal partner for Sovkino in the agreements creating Derussa.[13]

Insofar as the course of negotiations which led to Derussa's founding can be reconstructed from the later testimony of the parties involved, the Soviets appear to have taken the initiative. The head of the Film and Photo Department at the Soviet Trade Commission, Edmund Zöhrer, suggested establishing a German subsidiary as an alternative to dealing with individual German distributors who were wary of the politics of Soviet filmmaking.[14] Julian Kaufmann, a Polish businessman who moved to Berlin after the war and became active in film import/export, acted for Sklarz, proposing the formal partnership in late 1926 and shouldering responsibility for working out its terms. In addition to negotiating with the Soviet Trade Commission in Berlin, Kaufmann made almost a dozen trips to Moscow in 1926–27, on at least one of which he was accompanied by Sklarz.[15] The contracts creating what was initially dubbed Derufa – the name was altered in the spring of 1928 – were settled in August and formalised in November 1927. Derussa's managerial team paired Zöhrer, from the Film and Photo

Department of the Trade Commission, with an experienced German distributor, Hermann Saklikower, himself the owner of Internationale Film-AG (IFA). Georg Sklarz was made chair of the board alongside Karl Begge, director of the Trade Commission.[16] For a period of three years Derussa received selection rights to Sovkino pictures and guaranteed Sovkino a minimum of US$7000 for each picture it accepted for distribution. Proceeds over this amount were to be split evenly between the partner firms; from its share Derussa was responsible for all distribution and advertising expenses.[17]

Although sale of Soviet films in Germany and beyond was the primary rationale for Derussa, the legislation which shielded the German film market from foreign (American) domination meant Derussa had to be more than a simple distribution arrangement. The quota law in effect in 1927 required proof of production or distribution of one domestic picture for each import permit.[18] Immediately after Derussa's founding the legislation was altered so that a fixed number of import certificates was shared in proportion to the number of German pictures distributed by each company in 1926 and 1927.[19] A fairly complex set of rules governed the transition from one quota system to the next, but the essential task remained. Since Derussa had contractual obligation to import a minimum of fifteen Russian pictures annually, it had to acquire, produce, or co-produce German pictures. Therefore, a supplementary contract regulated the production or acquisition of 'quota films': each was to cost about 100,000 marks and be cost-shared between the contracting parties. For this purpose Derussa hired a production supervisor, Rudolf Meinert, and planned its own production programme.[20] It also contracted with third parties to produce some of its films, a common practice in the German film industry.

In addition to regulating the acquisition of quota films, the Derussa deal included a contract which detailed terms for joint Soviet–German production. Co-productions were to satisfy quota requirements, that is, they were to qualify as German films, but in style and appearance they were to be Russian. Exterior scenes were first to be done in the Soviet Union; interior shots were then slated for Staaken. Screenplays needed to be approved by the Russian censor before production could

begin.[21] Each side in the agreement assumed responsibility for the portion of the picture produced within its jurisdiction. Cost estimates had to be separated accordingly so that any overruns were charged to the responsible party rather than shared between them. Ultimately two negatives were to be completed, respecting the 'special characteristics' of each country. Sovkino had distribution rights in the Soviet Union; Derussa those for Germany. Once Staaken covered its production costs, proceeds in Germany, as elsewhere outside the Soviet Union, were to be split evenly.[22]

In its main outlines the partnership of Staaken and Sovkino cannot be described as novel. Various German–American combinations of similar structure had been formed in preceding years to exchange cost-sharing for import permits.[23] Nonetheless, even though Derussa lacked the ideological commitment on the German side which underpinned IAH and Prometheus, it had a unique dimension. Since Sovkino was a state company, represented abroad by the Trade Commission, which in turn co-managed Derussa through its representative, Zöhrer, there was an official investment of prestige as well as funding in Derussa. The willingness of Sovkino to sign such a pact signalled to German trade circles that the Soviet Union was emerging from cinematic isolation and was prepared to create pictures suitable for export.[24] Expressions of goodwill reflected the great expectations derived from this development and from the prevailing prestige of Soviet cinema. Derussa's logo, a bracelet joined by the image of a handshake, captured the spirit of cooperation.

Since between its imports and quota pictures Derussa projected distribution of 30 feature films annually, it had aspirations to rank among the handful of larger German distributors. To realise such an ambitious programme the new firm required substantial outlays in two main areas:

(1) distribution – to establish branch offices in each of the five regions into which Germany was divided and to support a major advertising campaign to break into the very competitive German market, and

(2) production – to finance the domestic productions and co-productions and/or purchase

Fig. 1. Boris Barnet's *Devuschka s korobkoi* (The Girl with a Hatbox, Mezhrabpom-Russ, 1927), anchored Derussa's first season of Soviet releases. It would prove to be the distributor's only Russian comedy.
[All photographs, Museum of Modern Art/Film Stills Archive.]

of distribution rights for other German pictures to meet quota requirements.

In conjunction with initial capital requirements Derussa therefore experienced a dual pressure to produce and distribute quickly; first, to generate revenue and second, to gain import certificates.

Acquiring import permits was absolutely essential for Derussa's survival. The task was complicated rather than eased by the change in regulations of late November 1927. As a new company, thus without films from 1926 and 1927 with which to earn a share of the quota, Derussa had immediately to begin production for the balance of the season 1927–28 and then finish these pictures by 30 April 1928 in order to qualify for compensation.[25] For subsequent seasons it needed to maintain a Ger-

man production schedule and, where unable to acquire an import licence through normal channels, attempt to purchase it (the market price was about 20,000 marks) from a limited pool of so-called export permits which could be legally traded. The demand for capital to sustain production/acquisition of films as well as the distribution apparatus was therefore unrelenting.[26]

Since Derussa began distribution late in the 1927–28 film season it opened with a truncated programme. When it staged its first premiere of Kozintsev and Trauberg's *Soiuz velikogo dela* (Union of the Great Deed, 1927), in February 1928, it was still in administrative embryo, advertising for sales representatives for regional distribution offices. In late February it released Pudovkin's *Konets Sankt-Peterburga* (The End of St Petersburg,

1927), but it was fully two months later that the third of its Soviet pictures, *Zemlia v plenu* (Earth in Chains, 1927), went into circulation. Its fourth and final Soviet premiere of the season, Boris Barnet's comedy *Devuschka s korobkoi* (The Girl with the Hatbox, 1928), came in mid-May.[27] By this time it had announced a programme of fifteen features (Russian and German) for the season 1928–29, among them Eisenstein's *Staroe i novoe/Generalnaia liniia* (The Old and the New – The General Line, 1929) and the first co-production, a spy tale to be directed by Abram Room starring Anna Sten, Alfred Abel, Bernhard Götzke, Fritz Kampers and Fritz Rasp.[28] In fact the company had a slow start. Only two Soviet pictures premiered before year's end, *Baby riazanskie* (Peasant Women of Riazan, 1927) and Evgenii Cherviakov's *Moi syn* (My Son, 1928); four more followed by late spring 1929. Co-production was postponed.

The first eighteen months after Derussa's founding appeared to mark steady progression toward its original goals. The company imported a dozen Soviet features, produced several pictures of its own and contracted for or acquired rights to the others required to meet its quota obligations. By early 1929 it was preparing to expand the partnership both with respect to the number of pictures it released and in terms of co-production. A Soviet delegation led by the chairman of Sovkino, Konstantin Shvedchikov, visited Berlin in March to organise co-productions and strengthen ties with German trade circles. Shvedchikov publicly confirmed that Sovkino was committed to enlarging its German sphere of influence through Derussa, particularly with the forthcoming collaborative projects. He also assured trade representatives that Soviet production would accommodate German demand for more light entertainment films as opposed to the heavier, problem-oriented pictures for which it was noted.[29] Several weeks after his departure he sent an open

Fig. 2. Trade advertisement for Derussa's release of *Zemlia v Plenu* (Earth in Chains/*Die Gelbe Pass*, 1927). *Der Film*, 1, 8 (May 1928): 17.

letter to German exhibitors thanking them for their warm reception of Soviet films and promising ongoing pursuit of excellence on the part of Soviet filmmakers and in the Sovkino–Derussa co-productions. In all of this Shvedchikov posed, like visiting American moguls, as a prophet of international understanding and exchange.[30]

Within a month of Shvedchikov's visit Derussa gave advance notice of two dozen releases for 1929–30. Heading its programme were three co-productions, the first of which, *Goroda i gody* (Cities and Years, 1930), was to be directed by Evgenii Cherviakov. Its domestic complement of

Fig. 3. *Oblomok imperii* (Fragment of an Empire, Sovkino, 1929), by Friedrich Ermler, was part of a strong Soviet programme which nevertheless failed to avert Derussa's sudden financial collapse.

In May the director of Sovkino, I.P. Trainin, was in Berlin to coordinate joint production. In an interview he hinted that the process of launching co-productions had not been easy, but that commitment to them was strong. He claimed that they would combine the best of German and Soviet cinema, offering both entertainment and relevant issues. No sacrifice of artistic integrity would be made, since Soviet film artists had demonstrated that the highest standards won public approval more than serial production of popular films. Significantly for what was to follow, Trainin denied that Soviet filmmakers deliberately created propaganda pictures; rather their dedication to art lent their work provocation and intensity.[32]

While Trainin was in Berlin came news of expansion on the international front. Thanks to the efforts of Georg Sklarz, Derussa and Filmwerke-Staaken were to join British Screen Productions and Rayart Pictures of New York in a British holding company, International Talking Screen Productions. This new firm boasted a massive capital base of £850,000 and was to acquire all Derussa's and Staaken's share capital. Although the partnership of Derussa and Sovkino was not to be materially affected by the transaction, the new arrangement promised to enhance the potential for Soviet distribution abroad and encourage German–Soviet co-production.[33]

To all outward appearances Derussa was about to reach its stride in 1929. Although its strategy in regard to the talking motion picture remained unresolved, its distribution programme

eleven features formed a cross-section of German production. Alongside three films starring Olga Tschechowa (Chekova), an emigré who made a career in Germany beginning after World War I, and two featuring the German Ellen Richter, were listed run-of-the-mill comedies and two action pictures starring Carlo Aldini. The Russian contribution comprised seven features, including Friedrich Ermler's *Oblomok imperii* (Fragment of an Empire, 1929), and three feature-length documentaries, foremost among the latter Dziga Vertov's *Chelovek s kinoappartom* (The Man with a Movie Camera, 1929).[31]

boasted a full complement of German and Soviet features; its international ties were broadened through International Talking Screen; its first co-production was scheduled to begin shooting in June. To outsiders, at least, it therefore came as a considerable shock when, in September, Derussa suspended payments and all its projects collapsed. Instead of fostering international understanding it left a trail of massive debts, the occasion for a lengthy, nasty battle over legal liability which set the Russian Trade Commission against Zöhrer and Sklarz.

Since Derussa's spectacular demise marked a watershed in German–Soviet film relations, the inescapable question for the historian is how the great expectations gave way to a financial debacle. The answer is largely contained in the legal proceedings, the exhaustive contemporary attempt to assess what went wrong. These proceedings were initiated by the Soviet Trade Commission in late August 1929 with a charge of fraud against Edmund Zöhrer. The charge cited an instance in August 1928 when Zöhrer received from the Commission 50,000 marks by terms of the co-financing agreement with Derussa but failed to deposit it into Derussa's account. When police questioned Zöhrer on the charge he acknowledged receipt of the money, likewise that it had by oversight not at first been entered into company books, but denied he pocketed the sum. Rather he used it, with the authorisation of Georg Sklarz, at his own discretion for promotional purposes.[34] The Trade Commission's response to Zöhrer's version of the transaction was that since the contract between itself and Derussa advanced funds only for production or acquisition of quota films, Zöhrer took the sum under false pretences. It also accused Zöhrer of breach of contract for accepting a second salary from Derussa in addition to that paid by itself.[35]

Given that Derussa suspended payments a week after the Trade Commission first called in the police, and that the second charge referred to Derussa's troubled finances, the initial charge reads as an attempt by the Trade Commission to wash its hands of Derussa's obligations. Certainly the larger question of financial liability formed the central issue in the ensuing legal case. Since the Trade Commission was represented on the managerial and supervisory boards of the company, it could

absolve itself only by pleading it had been duped, thus by charging Zöhrer with breach of trust and fraud and simultaneously incriminating Georg Sklarz.[36]

The judicial investigation quickly gained a much wider compass when Derussa proved incapable of satisfying its creditors. An initial trustee's audit revealed that the 50,000 marks charged against Zöhrer was truly pocket-money: uncovered debt stood at almost 2,900,000 marks. In a lengthy report with multiple addenda, the trustee concluded that Derussa was in trouble within months of its creation, largely because it assumed enormous obligations for quota pictures which were box office failures. Inflated operating costs, unfavourable film contracts and expensive borrowing policy combined to bury the company. What remained to be determined was whether criminal charges were justified. That determination would depend upon a painstaking review of company financial records which the trustee described as tangled and incomplete.[37]

Trade papers, hitherto generally supportive of Derussa, did not wait for the attorney general's conclusions to charge foul play. Sensitive to the accusation that the film industry accommodated shady dealers, they were quick to disown Sklarz and associates as outsiders whose business practices had long been notorious.[38] That Derussa could accumulate such debts in less than two years constituted proof enough that its management was incompetent and underhanded. Significantly, however, trade opinion laid ultimate responsibility for the debacle at the door of the Trade Commission. Since the Commission was represented on the supervisory board of the company it had obviously been derelict in its duty to provide financial oversight. Moreover, film circles maintained that Derussa's fate had broader implications for Soviet trade with the West. Derussa's credit-worthiness and reliability as a distributor had been dependent from the start on its backing by the Trade Commission, for on the Soviet side Derussa had clearly been an official company. The efforts of the Commission to deny this reality and pose as a creditor of Derussa rather than as a guarantor for its debts threatened to undermine whatever confidence other firms had in the Soviets as trading partners.[39]

The first accountant assigned to disentangle

Derussa's financial history produced an indictment of company management consistent with trade opinion. It charged corruption, fraud and mismanagement at every turn: salaries were judged extravagant, operational costs out of line, film purchases unrealistic or downright fraudulent, and borrowing arrangements catastrophic. But in its zeal to convict and unfamiliarity with motion picture business this report quickly betrayed its own superficiality. Under questioning by the investigating judge the accountant responsible for it confessed that he had ducked the labyrinthine problems posed by Derussa's irregular bookkeeping by entrusting the task to two assistants. He then only skimmed their report, trusting the attorney general's office to sort out the mess.[40]

A second expert assigned to the case qualified or dismissed most of the criminal charges but concurred with the general tenor of the trustee's audit that Derussa's finances collapsed as a result of mismanagement. Derussa invested far more in operational costs and film purchases, at high interest charges, than it recovered from Sovkino's advances and gross film receipts; simply put, overhead exceeded cash flow. If and where criminal liability applied remained exceedingly hard to pinpoint.[41] Despite much prodding from the Ministry of Justice the investigation got bogged down by financial complexities and the tangle of charges and counter-charges.[42] Combined with delays caused by the need to call in the second accounting expert, these meant that the formal indictment was not ready until June 1931. Charges were then laid against Zöhrer and another manager of Derussa, Cornell Pop, for breach of trust and fraud.[43] Attempts to stage a trial in 1932 were frustrated when Pop elected to stay abroad rather than return to stand trial. When the case against Zöhrer was called separately in 1933 he had already left Germany for Czechoslovakia. Sklarz, a key witness, was in Paris. Neither could anticipate friendly treatment from Nazi justice and they chose not to return. The whole matter languished and was finally struck from the court files in 1939.[44]

Although the legal case never found resolution, the investigation produced an illuminating history of Derussa's road to ruin. Set within the context of the economic challenges facing the film industry in the late 1920s this history acquires a logic which

the initial outrage over Derussa's debts obscured. Overly optimistic visions, competing agendas and the pressure for rapid expansion combined with poor management to undermine what initially appeared a viable cinematic bridge between Germany and the Soviet Union.

Finding credit in a highly competitive and congested market was the central task of German film production after the great inflation. Several larger firms acquired assistance from American partners; smaller firms remained so primarily for lack of capital to fund expansion.[45] Since Derussa was obliged to cover operating costs from distribution income, but had to produce domestically to import the Russian pictures required to generate that income, it needed some early box office favourites to balance the books. The beginnings showed promise: company records reveal that the second and third Soviet pictures it distributed – *The End of St Petersburg* and *Earth in Chains* – proved the most successful of all its releases. There is evidence, however, that these early successes fed already unrealistic revenue projections, which from the start contributed to administrative extravagance and extremely risky borrowing policy. Salaries and related expenses were inflated, and in the expectation of further profits from sales in western Europe the company expanded far more rapidly than its later distribution results could justify.[46]

No one cause can be identified for the gap between expenditure and revenue, but crushing losses appeared in the results for Derussa's domestic production. In one regard Derussa was in good company: quota pictures normally represented minimal profit. Although they rarely served only to gain an import permit – to be shelved rather than exhibited – their primary rationale was to admit a foreign film. In another respect, however, Derussa's experience was anomalous, since quota pictures were also not to consume much funding. By the terms of its agreement with Sovkino, the German feature films were not normally to cost more than 100,000 marks, a modest sum at the time. In fact, though usually targeted for sums less than these, Derussa's pictures frequently experienced overruns.[47]

The most damaging and controversial debit column among the quota pictures came from the purchase of seven features from Sklarz's own

Phönix-Film A.G. at a cost of 1.115 million marks, with an eighth to follow for an additional 200,000 marks. Given the high cost of these films and the potential conflict of interest for Sklarz, judicial investigators examined this transaction very closely. To their questioning Cornell Pop openly confessed that the deal disadvantaged Derussa because the Phönix productions carried inflated price tags, made doubly burdensome by the fact that several of the films were already in circulation when sold and thus of diminished box office potential for Derussa. Sklarz defended himself on the grounds that he was abroad at the time of the purchase, while also claiming that the Phönix features were contract films into whose planning and personnel Derussa had direct input. Since they were produced to meet Derussa's quota requirements he dismissed the issue of cost as irrelevant. Neither Pop nor Sklarz had a fully satisfactory rationale for a deal which, as the trustee's report concluded, appeared rigged to transfer financial liability for overpriced films from

Fig. 4. Derussa did serve as a main channel to the west for Soviet cinema. This still from Pudovkin's *Konyets Sankt-Peterburga* (The End of St. Petersburg, Mezhrabpom-Russ, 1927), distributed to publicise the film's opening in New York, retains the German title which Derussa printed into the negative.

Phönix via Derussa to the Soviets through the cost-sharing agreement.[48] The pressure to meet quota requirements figured prominently in this transaction, especially for Zöhrer, who would otherwise have been concerned to safeguard Soviet interests against those of Sklarz's Phönix-Film. With these eight films Derussa immediately gained a domestic track record upon which to acquire import permits.[49]

Had these German pictures justified their inflated costs with strong theatre runs the net effect could still have been favourable. In fact, however, most of them distinguished themselves by unusually dismal box office receipts. The majority did not even

begin to cover their costs, let alone turn a modest profit. Losses on the pictures acquired from Phönix-Film alone totalled 325,000 marks, almost equivalent to Sovkino's advance to Derussa of 50,000 marks per picture. By tying up enormous amounts of capital in unremunerative pictures Derussa found itself pressed into borrowing at extortionate rates in order to keep itself afloat. On a number of occasions it took loans or had to have bills of exchange discounted at rates close to one per cent per day – i.e. over 300 per cent annually.[50]

Catastrophic results with domestic pictures left the company's revenue expectations overwhelmingly dependent upon the Sovkino imports. Gener-

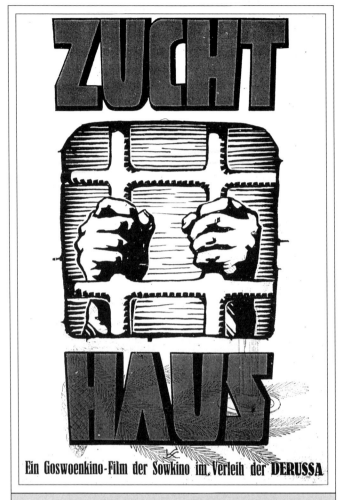

Fig. 5. Trade advertisement for Derussa's release of *Katorga* (Penal Servitude/*Zuchthaus*, 1928). *Der Film*, vol. 23 (Christmas 1928): 15.

parts, failing to recover even the very modest cost of licence and copies. On balance then, Derussa's Soviet pictures did not capture German movie-goers and certainly did not fulfill the hopes invested in them in 1927.[51]

Derussa's distribution misfortunes were hardly unique in the film world, where miscalculations and the shifting preferences of the movie-going public shredded entrepreneurial hopes. What distinguished them was their repercussions on a company which paired an official institution from a socialist country with private enterprise. With the best intentions on both sides, tension between Derussa's and Sovkino's objectives was all but inevitable. That tension surfaced in the very different versions of Derussa's history offered by the Soviet Trade Commission and the company managers. Whereas the Trade Commission accused Zöhrer, Sklarz *et al.* of capitalist excesses – self-serving, fraudulent business dealings – the accused, while admitting mistakes, charged Sovkino and the Trade Commission with communist excesses – doctrinaire adherence to political as opposed to commercial goals. They argued that they had done what was possible under circumstances made unbearable by lack of support or outright obstruction from Sovkino and the Trade Commission.

The key individuals in this counterattack were Zöhrer and Sklarz. More than any other person Zöhrer was familiar with, and responsible for, the internal workings of the company. He had also had to straddle the awkward divide between Soviet and German interests. Though of Austrian background, he had proven himself a loyal official of the Soviet Union. Viennese by birth and a volunteer in 1914 at the age of eighteen, Zöhrer became a prisoner-of-war in Siberia. When the Russian Revolution brought his release he joined the Communist Party and fought with the Red Army in Manchuria. After

ally speaking these did somewhat better, managing to avoid red ink, but only because their normal acquisition cost of $7,000 dollars (29,4000 marks) each was only a fraction of production expenditure for the average quota film. Their earnings did not begin to make good the enormous drain from administrative extravagance and losses on the quota pictures. There was nothing even remotely paralleling the smash success of *Battleship Potemkin,* which allegedly grossed 900,000 marks. Only two pictures, *The End of St Petersburg* and *Earth in Chains,* earned between 150,000 and 200,000 marks. All the others earned just over 100,000 or less; several proved no more popular than their German counter-

being assigned to organise a revolutionary army in Germany for the national uprising anticipated there in 1920–21, he became governor of a district in Siberia, where he served until 1926. Called to Berlin he functioned as assistant manager of the Economic Department of the Trade Commission before appointment as head of the Film and Photo Department.[52]

According to Zöhrer, German–Soviet film trade was in a sorry state at the time of his appointment in December 1926. Apart from the success of *Potemkin*, which he attributed mainly to the censorship controversy, the Trade Commission had little to show for its film efforts. Despite the proceeds from *Potemkin*, it was owed about one million marks by Prometheus. Since his appointment coincided with instructions from Moscow to its foreign representatives to enhance the international profile of Soviet cinema, and since Berlin was the distribution centre for Soviet films in the western world, Zöhrer's task was to make a name for Soviet cinema abroad and to lead the Film and Photo Department out of the red. He claimed that his three-year tenure at the Trade Commission yielded a quantum leap in international sales and healthy profits. It certainly corresponded to the high point of international interest in Soviet cinema.[53]

With respect to Derussa, Zöhrer argued that Sovkino and the Trade Commission hindered more than they helped. Sovkino promised special productions, apolitical in nature and geared for export, but failed to deliver them. Most of its offerings were propaganda pictures. In addition, Sovkino did not honor its commitment to supply 50 per cent of the funds required to make the quota films. Zöhrer was therefore dependent upon the financial backing of Sklarz and his own promotional efforts with exhibitors across Europe to sell Soviet films. From this perspective Zöhrer and Sklarz became paired in a desperate struggle to make Derussa profitable despite being left in the lurch by Sovkino.[54]

Georg Sklarz essentially endorsed Zöhrer's criticisms, even while claiming that Zöhrer had blackmailed him into bad deals and had squeezed him out of the day-to-day operations of the company in September 1928.[55] Sklarz's version of Derussa's history combined grand visions for German–Soviet cooperation and charges of betrayal by Sovkino.

His expectation of huge profits was rooted in three factors:

(1)   the achievements and reputation of Soviet filmmakers,

(2)   joint production, equivalent to access to the Russian market, and

(3)   prospects for European-wide distribution.

The first of these he took, very optimistically, as grounds for anticipating unusually high box office receipts – a minimum gross of 300,000 marks – from German release of major Sovkino pictures. The second he registered, with some justification, as a distinct advantage for Derussa's co-productions which, unlike the normal quota films, were to be big-budget pictures. Although Sovkino had exclusive claim to Soviet earnings, and a 50 per cent claim on receipts elsewhere, Sklarz saw co-production as the Soviets subsidising motion pictures that would win international acclaim as well as sell at home. Derussa had the opportunity to compete abroad at half the cost of firms lacking such an alliance.[56]

Sale of co-productions in western Europe presented the most tantalising of Sklarz's ambitions. From shortly after Derussa's founding he focused his energy on creating a European network for financing as well as distributing the co-productions. His scheme was simple – to relieve Derussa of its share of production costs by procuring advances on distribution rights in other countries. From early 1928 until September 1929 he spent most of his time abroad in pursuit of this vision.[57] With Filmwerke-Staaken as his financial base – valued, he claimed, at over nine million marks – and the lure of Soviet filmic achievements, he negotiated cost-sharing subcontracts with companies in France, Italy, Spain and England. He managed, for instance, to sell French distribution rights for the first projected co-production to the Société Générale des Films in Paris for a guarantee of 200,000 marks, more than the Derussa share of its estimated budget of 370,000 marks. He also negotiated the deal with International Talking Screen Productions. In short, Sklarz laid the groundwork for integration of German–Soviet collaboration into a pan-European bloc in which large-scale productions would be financed by multiple partners.[58]

Sklarz admitted that his European scheme remained embryonic, since no co-production had yet materialised.[59] But he also saw it as unassailable so long as production went forward. He, like Zöhrer, therefore rationalised defeat in political rather than commercial terms: in pursuit of assured profits he was stabbed in the back by Sovkino, which stalled on co-productions and delivered propaganda films rather than the broadly conceived entertainment features which it promised. Looking back, Sklarz suspected a propaganda ploy in the whole partnership. When Derussa exercised its contractual right to reject political pictures Sovkino dragged its feet on co-productions. Derussa then came under immense pressure to find or produce quota films to give it something to distribute. Its schemes for European cost-sharing of joint productions also failed to get off the ground. Eventually it had little choice but to accept Sovkino propaganda for distribution.[60]

The charge that political machinations ruined Derussa became the main point of contention in an arbitration case which ran parallel to the criminal investigation. This case rested on a personal guarantee Sklarz had been obliged to give the Soviets in 1927 in order to get them to finalise the deal with Staaken. The Russians now invoked the guarantee to press a claim for compensation of about 150,000 marks.[61] Sklarz's attempt to annul their claim revolved around the terms of the initial agreement and the definition of political filmmaking. He, like Zöhrer, insisted that the deal specifically promised Derussa apolitical feature films – though they both admitted that this promise had been verbal, since the Soviet Communist Party would not have approved a contract containing written assurance of the same. He also clearly judged as propaganda not only pictures glorifying the revolution but also historical dramas and contemporary society films in which good and evil were apportioned according to class lines and political allegiance.[62]

Soviet officials flatly denied knowledge of, or complicity in, a verbal agreement circumventing the authority of the Communist Party. Not surprisingly, they claimed unwavering loyalty to the Party and its regulations. But they also cited a peculiar perspective on politics and the cinema. The Soviet film bosses pretended ignorance of the difference between a political and apolitical film. In their formu-

lation a promise not to export political pictures made no sense since the very term lacked meaning to them. Their plea was not, of course, a personal one, but an obligatory, Stalinist statement about the unity of culture and politics. They consistently maintained, against the combined testimony of Sklarz, Zöhrer and Kaufmann, that such an issue had never been raised in negotiations for the deal or in subsequent correspondence between Derussa and Sovkino.[63]

This *ex post facto* reading of Soviet cinema in the 1920s obliterated the past, in fine Stalinist fashion, to serve the present. In particular it elided the fierce Soviet debates of the second half of the 1920s between the protagonists of popular cinema – 'export films' – and ideologues who wanted film to enlighten the masses. While the cause of Derussa's demise cannot be reduced to sabotage from the Soviet side, the company's existence did coincide with a fundamental shift in Soviet motion picture priorities. When Derussa was founded, Sovkino, though already facing criticism from the 'enlighteners', championed popular entertainment capable of challenging foreign domination of the Russian market. Drawing on the experience of earlier box office hits from Mezhrabpom, Sovkino managed to redress the balance against foreign (American) domination of Soviet theatres and raise export earnings.[64] Yet precisely as Derussa's first releases were shown in Germany the tide turned decisively against commercial ('bourgeois' or 'export') cinema. The Party Conference on Cinema in March 1928 marked the beginning of the Cultural Revolution in film. Henceforth the motion picture was to participate in and serve the larger cause of building socialism in one country. Moreover, foreign films, perceived as a source of corruption and a waste of valuable foreign exchange, were squeezed out of the Soviet market. By the summer of that year Sovkino had begun to trim its sails to the new wind.[65] Although it still managed to produce a number of pictures that satisfied the requirements of entertainment and enlightenment, it came under increasing pressure prior to its liquidation in 1930.[66]

When questioned closely about these developments, Soviet cinema officials combined double-talk and counter-attack. The term 'export film' was dismissed by Shvedchikov just as decisively as the term 'political film'. With remarkable disingenuousness he defined export films as those which the Soviet censor approved for sale abroad – as though the Soviet censor were a non-political agency. He admitted that there had been strong press polemics in 1928–29 against the films allegedly produced for export, but downplayed these as the opinions of individual critics which were not binding on filmmakers. When asked whether these impacted the types of films Derussa received he professed inability to see any point to the question![67]

The counter-attack addressed more specifically the context within which Derussa had been founded, insisting that Sklarz and Zöhrer were guilty of their own foreshortening of the past. The Soviets maintained that the reference point for negotiations in 1926–27 was primarily *Battleship Potemkin*. Only the blind could dismiss the political thrust of the picture; and only the most doctrinaire anticommunist distributor would have refused a repeat of *Potemkin's* box office. Shvedchikov conceded that Sklarz and Kaufmann had mentioned other types of films in talks prior to signing the contract, but that focus had been on *Potemkin*. In short, given the type of Soviet picture which first captured German attention, an understanding not to export political films would have been unusual indeed.[68]

The rejoinder from Sklarz and Zöhrer aimed to expose the fault line in Soviet filmmaking which Shvedchikov denied existed. In place of *Potemkin* they cited two very popular melodramas of mid-decade, also distributed in Germany in 1926, as the point of departure for their expectations at Derussa's founding. *Medvezhia svadba* (The Bear's Wedding, 1925) was a suspenseful rendering of the vampire motif co-scripted by Anatolii Lunacharskii, the Commissar of Enlightenment. *Kollezhskii registrator* (The Station Master, 1926), based on a short story by Pushkin, chronicled the passion of a wealthy officer for the daughter of a minor official. Neither had political significance other than as representatives of social and entertainment values which the revolution aimed to eliminate.[69]

Potemkin and *The Bear's Wedding* stand conveniently as polar opposites in contemporary debate. The pictures Derussa actually accepted for German distribution largely fell between these poles and in this regard comprised a broad cross-section of Soviet production. At one end of the

spectrum, *The End of St Petersburg* represented the political commitment for which Soviet cinema was noted. Beside it were ranged several historical pictures of explicit political context such as *Novyi Vavilon* (The New Babylon, 1929) on the Paris commune of 1871, and *Union of the Great Deed*. Social issues with political overtones were treated in *Katorga* (Penal Servitude, 1928), which dealt with penitentiary conditions under the tsarist regime, *The Peasant Women of Riazan* (oppression of women in village life) and *Earth in Chains* (prostitution). *Sorok pervyi* (The Forty-first, 1927), directed by Iakov Protazanov, presented a romantic conflict against the dramatic backdrop of the Civil War. In addition to several documentaries there was also one comedy among the dozen Soviet pictures Derussa released: Boris Barnet's *The Girl with the Hat Box*.

Derussa's Russian imports cannot therefore be lumped together as propaganda pictures. If any generic label applies it is the one admitted by both Shvedchikov and Trainin, namely, heaviness and issue-orientation as opposed to light diversion and amusement. With few exceptions, such as Barnet's *The Girl with the Hatbox*, the heavy melodrama of pre-revolutionary Russian cinema persisted in the Soviet era, whether political issues were dominant or recessive. By that token, though *Battleship Potemkin* and *The End of St Petersburg* did not set the tone, neither did *The Bear's Wedding* and *The Station Master*. From this perspective Derussa's Soviet pictures fell between two stools, capitalising neither on the sex, violence and suspense of Lunacharskii's *The Bear's Wedding* nor on the revolutionary zeal and stylistic verve of Eisenstein's classic. Moreover, box office results did not speak unequivocally for or against one film genre. Barnet's comedy and Protazanov's romantic drama both grossed less than 50,000 marks.[70]

The high financial stakes and bad feeling attached to the Derussa affair made debate over the boundaries between political and commercial cinema, historically problematic enough, particularly acrimonious. In retrospect one must qualify the claims of both parties. Contrary to the vehement denials of Stalin's minions, Soviet cinema did recognise film genres familiar to the West, both historically and because movie-goers and film experts alike were familiar with German and American

Fig. 6. *Novyi Vavilon (The New Babylon*, Sovkino, 1929). Kozintsev and Trauberg's film was sold to German audiences as a Prussian national epic, with disastrous results [Museum of Modern Art/Film Stills Archive].

production. Statements from Soviet film bosses visiting Berlin clearly indicate that they understood the demands of the German box office and aimed to serve them. Finally, Soviet production displayed considerable variety. However political or social in general orientation – filmmaking without reference to concrete circumstances is difficult in any context – Soviet cinema drew on traditional and foreign precedents as well as developing its own identity.[71]

On the German side, differentiation between political and commercial pictures was initially less definitive than Sklarz or Kaufmann maintained. At stake was much less the political clash provoked by Bolshevik glorification of revolt in films like *Battleship Potemkin* than the long-term critical and audience response to the style and ethos of Soviet production. Distributors and critics, taken by surprise with *Battleship Potemkin*, tended to identify Soviet cinema with Eisenstein and Pudovkin. Indeed, the early success of these directors lent Soviet cinema an artistic mystique which persisted through the end of the decade.[72] Despite Sovkino's intent to diversify its production to win foreign viewers, that mystique had distinctly political overtones. One of Germany's most perceptive and prolific critics, Roland Schacht, commented a full year after *Potemkin* that all Russian films appeared to be 'Tendenzfilme'. Critical respect for the relationship between cinematic innovation and reordering of Russian state and society did not, however, remove concern for the marketability of the Soviet product. In mid-1929 another expert, Hans Pander, challenged Soviet cinema to escape its revolutionary rut:

> The demand among non-Russian countries for such films from the period of the Russian revolution can be considered long since met. It's time that the Russians turn to other motifs which aren't drawn from the narrow circle of Russian issues but treat more general human affairs. Whether they are capable of this remains to be proven.[73]

The reaction against political impulses grew as Soviet cinematic techniques became familiar and great works came fewer and farther between. Politically motivated portrayal of good and evil became especially obtrusive. A review of *The End of St Petersburg* noting 'black versus white portraiture presented with the naivety of wild west drama' indicates that Soviet cinema encountered critical resistance just like American films which were mocked for gross simplification of moral conflicts.[74] When such moralising was paired with obsessive symbolism and confusingly executed plots, that resistance hardened. *New Babylon,* the last Sovkino feature released by Derussa before the criminal investigation began in 1929, offers a case in point. This tale set in the Paris Commune, directed by Leonid Trauberg and Grigorii Kozintsev, stirred intense controversy in the Soviet Union for its formalist and experimental qualities.[75] According to Sklarz it was offered to Derussa as a film about Prussia's defeat of France in 1870–71 with extensive scenes of Prussian troops. On this understanding Derussa launched an extensive advertising campaign. But instead of a German national epic Sovkino delivered a 'Communist propaganda film of the crudest kind' in which every second title proclaimed 'long live the revolution'.[76] Sklarz was not alone in reacting to its crass political dichotomies. One socialist reviewer branded it the epitome of Soviet cinema's distorted world view: 'instead of history, propaganda; instead of dialectic, black and white contrasts; instead of characterisation, caricature; instead of acting, ballet; instead of faces, grimaces; instead of art, hysterics.'[77]

While *New Babylon* presents an extreme case, it highlights a trend in German reception of Soviet cinema which, in retrospect, is not terribly surprising. In 1926 *Battleship Potemkin* took Germany by storm. A number of subsequent imports, such as *Mat'* (Mother, 1926) and *Potomok Chingiz-khana* (Storm over Asia, 1928) – won similar accolades, if not the box office return of *Potemkin*.[78] For a time reputation alone carried considerable weight. Otherwise, the Soviet Union, like Hollywood before it, did not have an endless store of creative products to sustain its reputation. Once the novelty wore off, and the political message became a growing irritant, revenue estimates proved overly optimistic. Even without the vitriolic domestic debate of the late 1920s Soviet cinema confronted a daunting challenge abroad. Although Derussa also came to ruin because its own productions or domestic purchases were expensive and unpopular, grandiose visions that Soviet pictures would conquer German theatres were simply unrealistic. In the long term the Soviets did not have a magic formula with which to outclass Hollywood and Berlin.

Viewed in light of developments in the Soviet Union, chances of long-term success were likewise dim. While the Cultural Revolution was scarcely foreseeable in 1926, any German firm with Soviet interests faced not only the usual hurdles of censorship and import restrictions but also possible political complications. To these must be added a perennial shortage of production capital, probably the underlying reason from the Soviet side for failure to pursue co-productions more energetically. On the heels of Derussa's establishment Soviet cinema experienced enormous upheaval with abandonment of the New Economic Policy and onset of Stalinisation. Simultaneously, the transition from silent to talking pictures, which drove up production costs as the depression brought a tightening of credit, raised the risks involved in film enterprise. Derussa's fate was not inevitable, but even had Sklarz and Zöhrer not been drawn (or forced, as they claimed) into extravagant adventures, German–Soviet film collaboration did not have a bright future.

Against this backdrop the commitment to Soviet–German cooperation expressed by Konstantin Shvedchikov and Ilia Trainin in Berlin in spring 1929 rings hollow. Certainly by the time the Trade Commission laid charges against Zöhrer in August 1929 the potential for Soviet film export, not to mention effective collaboration for co-productions, had shrunk enormously. Quite apart from the significant hurdles presented by the transition to talking film, the kind and number of motion pictures produced in Soviet Russia by 1930 would have left Derussa stranded.[79] From this perspective the Trade Commission's pose as a creditor duped by Derussa's management suggests that the Soviets had already decided collaboration was unsustainable. The criminal charges can be read as an attempt to recoup losses and run.

None of this exculpates Derussa's management from dealings ranging from misguided to fraudulent, but it suggests there is rough justice in the fact that the Soviet Trade Commission's charges against Zöhrer and Derussa management never brought convictions. From mid-1928 at the latest, Sovkino's domestic position was not one which could sustain meaningful ties with a western partner like Derussa. Soviet resistance to the import of German pictures presented a further obstacle to long-term ties with foreign companies. The Soviet Union was entering a period of intense self-preoccupation, as industrialisation and collectivisation impacted all aspects of Soviet life. In the last two years of the 'Golden Age' of Soviet cinema the German–Russian Film Alliance had a defensible rationale, even if it largely failed in its essential purposes. By 1929 its raison d'être had passed into history. ♣

Acknowledgement

The research for this article was made possible by a grant from the Social Sciences and Humanities Research Council of Canada. I am indebted as well to Denise J. Youngblood for her critical comments and suggestions.

Notes

1. For recent scholarship exploring these links see the catalogue to the exhibit *Berlin-Moskau, 1900–50* (Munich: Prestel, 1995); Eduard Ditschek, *Politisches Engagement und Medienexperiment: Theater und Film der russischer und deutscher Avantgarde der 20er Jahre* (Tübingen: Günter Narr, 1989).

2. The early industry ties are covered in Kristin Thompson, 'Government Policies and Practical Necessities in the Soviet Cinema of the 1920s, in Anna Lawton, ed., *The Red Screen* (London & New York: Routledge, 1992), 19–41. Cf. Vance Kepley, Jr, 'The Origins of Soviet Cinema: A Study in Industry Development', in Ian Christie & Richard Taylor, eds., *Inside the Film Factory* (London: Routledge, 1991), 60–79. On Soviet exports see Denise Hartsough, 'Soviet Film Distribution and Exhibition in Germany, 1921–33', *Historical Journal of Film, Radio and Television*, 5 (1985): 131–48.

3. Introduction to Oksana Bulgakowa, ed., *Die ungewöhnlichen Abenteuer des Dr. Mabuse im Lande der Bolschewiki* (Berlin: Freunde der Deutschen Kinemathek, 1995), 7. For more on the proliferation of formal and informal links, particularly between the Russian and German film avant-garde, see Jörg Schöning, ed., *Fantaisies Russes. Russische Film-macher in Berlin und Paris 1920–30* (Munich: edition text + kritik, 1995).

4. From a substantial literature on Münzenberg and Prometheus cf. Vance Kepley, Jr, 'The Workers International Relief and the Cinema of the Left 1921–35', *Cinema Journal*, 23 (1983): 7–23; Babette Gross, *Willi Münzenberg: A Political Biography* (Ann Arbor: Michigan State University Press, 1974); Rolf Surmann, *Die Münzenberg-Legende* (Cologne: Prometh, 1983); Bruce Murray, *Film and the German Left in the Weimar Republic* (Austin: University of Texas Press, 1990), ch. 10. Also see Hartsough, 'Soviet Film Distribution', and Jörg Schöning, 'Vom Russen-Club zum Russenkult', in Schöning, ed., *Fantaisies Russes*, 26.

5. Full details are in Alexander Jason, *Handbuch der Filmwirtschaft* (Berlin: Verlag für Presse, Wirtschaft und Politik, 1930), vol. 2, 160ff. *Medvezhia Svadba* (The Bear's Wedding, 1925), *Aelita* (1924) and *Kollezhskii registrator* (The Station Master, 1926) were handled by Lloydkino; *Tret'ia Meshchanskai* (Bed and Sofa, 1927) by Südfilm, *Mat'* (Mother, 1926) by Hirschel-Sofar. On the variety of German companies which exported to the Soviet Union see Thompson, 'Government Policies'.

6. Bulgakowa, 'Russische Filme in Berlin', in *Die ungewöhnlichen Abenteuer des Dr. Mabuse*, 81, confuses Derussa with Deruss of 1922; Alexander Bloch, a bookkeeper, is named head of the company, presumably because falsely identified with the emigré director, Noé [Alexander] Bloch. Hartsough, 'Soviet Film Distribution', 139, mentions Derussa only in passing, though a number of Soviet titles distributed by Derussa appear in her text. Murray, *Film and the German Left*, 130, 137, does the same. Thompson, 'Government Policies', 39, notes the firm as an unwritten chapter in German–Soviet film ties.

7. For original documents and opinion on the censorship controversy see G. Kuhn *et al.*, eds., *Film und revolutionäre Arbeiterbewegung in Deutschland, 1918–32* (Berlin: Henschelverlag, 1975), vol. 1, 323–69.

8. Germany's progressive critics cited it as evidence that cinematic innovation did not signify minimal box office appeal. On this theme see Kristin Thompson, 'Eisenstein's Early Films Abroad', in Ian Christie & Richard Taylor, eds., *Eisenstein Rediscovered* (London: Routledge, 1993), 53–63, here especially 55–59.

9. Kepley, 'The Origins of Soviet Cinema', 73–75.

10. Richard Taylor, *The Politics of the Soviet Cinema, 1917–29* (Cambridge: Cambridge University Press, 1979), 87–101. German appreciation of

tension in Soviet cinema objectives prior to announcement of Derussa's establishment is evidenced in 'Russische Filmhoffnungen', *Lichtbildbühne* (31 August 1927).

11. With Helphand he also mass-produced calendars for Russia which never found their market. There is some information on these dealings in Z.A.B. Zeman, *The Merchant of Revolution: The Life of Alexander Israel Helphand (Parvus)* (London: Oxford University Press, 1965), 196–205.

12. The nastiness of the campaign against the Sklarz family can be sampled in the pseudonymous pamphlet: Sincton Upclair, *Der Rattenkönig: Revolutions-Schieber und ihre Helfer* (Berlin: Fr. Warthemann, 1920).

13. On the Staaken studio see Uta Berg-Ganschow & Wolfgang Jacobsen, *... Film ... Stadt ... Kino ... Berlin ...* (Berlin: Argon, 1987), 173–76, 195–97. Rent at each of the five studios in the Staaken complex was reported as 2,000 marks daily, which would give credence to contemporary claims that Sklarz was personally very wealthy when Derussa was founded. See Peter Sachse, 'Ein Film-Tag in Staaken', *Berliner Mittagszeitung (Das kleine Journal)* (4 December 1927).

14. See the testimony of Zöhrer in Landesarchiv Berlin, Rep. 58, Acc. 399, no. 2676 [henceforth LAB 58/2676], vol. 3, 49. Sklarz had apparently already acted on behalf of Sovkino through Staaken to mediate export of Soviet films. See ibid., vol. 2, 201, for Sklarz's confirmation that the Russians approached him.

15. Cf. his statement of 14 March 1930 in ibid., vol. 2, 39–42, and vol. 7, Anlage I.

16. See the press release from Derussa: 'Deutsch-russische Film-Allianz', *Der Film* (15 October 1927), 24; 'Deutsch–russische Kombination', *Reichsfilmblatt*, no. 41 (1927): 42.

17 See LAB 58/2676, vol. 1, 186–93.

18. Hartsough, 'Soviet Film Distribution', 131, notes the problems posed by German censorship and taxation, but neither hurdle rivalled that raised by the import quota. Zöhrer described acquisition of import permits a matter of life and death for the company.

19. The new law is reproduced in 'Einfuhrregelung für die Kontingentsperiode 1927–28', *Der Film* (1 December 1927), 27.

20. See LAB 58/2676, vol. I, 180, and the submission from the Trade Commission's lawyer in ibid., 39–45.

21. Germany did not have this form of precensorship until the Third Reich.

22. See LAB 58/2676, vol. 1, 181–85. An addendum specified that Derussa was liable for any failure of these pictures to recover their production costs.

23. See Thomas Saunders, *Hollywood in Berlin* (Berkeley: University of California Press, 1994), 81. For the close parallels between Derussa and contracts for Mezhrabpom, including that for co-productions, cf. Jekaterina Chochlowa (Ekaterina Khokhlova), 'Mezhrabpom. Dokumente', in Bulgakowa, ed., *Die ungewöhnliche Abenteuer*, 195–97.

24. Leading trade papers offered generous, friendly coverage. See 'Eine russisch-deutsche Filmgemeinschaft', *Film Express* (October/November 1927), 27–29; *Lichtbildbühne* (13 October 1927), for a lengthy interview with Zöhrer which editorialised that Derussa represented a significant departure in Soviet film policy, demonstrating, through willingness to co-finance German pictures to make export possible, a shift from self-preoccupation to international, commercial cinema. 'Der Ifa-Sovkino-Vertrag', *Film-Kurier* (11 October 1927), concurred that Derussa marked a new phase in Soviet Russia's international film trade.

25. Terms governing transition from the old system to the new are in 'Kontingent 1928–29', *Lichtbildbühne* (25 November 1927).

26. Zöhrer explained the relevance of quota regulations in a long submission to the court of 6 January 1930 in LAB 58/2676, vol. 1, 158–66.

27. Zöhrer later claimed five Soviet releases in the first season: see 'Rußland und wir', *Lichtbildbühne* (26 September 1928).

28. See *Film-Kurier* (4 June 1928); *Lichtbildbühne* (6 July 1928).

29. Expressions of faith in German–Soviet collaboration were combined with an appeal for easing of the quota restrictions on the import of Soviet films. See 'Sowkino wünscht Kontingent-Erleichterung', *Lichtbildbühne* (15 March 1929); 'Schwedschikows Dank an die deutsche Filmindustrie', ibid. (22 March 1929); 'Die deutschen Kinobesitzer schätzen den Russenfilm', *Film-Kurier* (22 March 1929).

30. The letter was published in *Film-Kurier* (17 April 1929).

31. See the large and detailed advertisement in *Lichtbildbühne* (20 April 1929), 1–10.

32. 'I. Trainin in Berlin', *Film-Kurier* (3 May 1929). The interview is 'Die Gemeinschaftsarbeit beginnt', ibid. (25 May 1929). For Trainin's advocacy of enter-

tainment cinema and interest in attracting foreign capital see Denise Youngblood, *Soviet Cinema in the Silent Era, 1918–35* (Austin: University of Texas Press, 1991), 37, 45–46, 82, 128.

33. 'Neuer internationaler Konzern', *Film-Kurier* (1 May 1929); 'International Talking Screen Productions Ltd.', *Lichtbildbühne* (11 May 1929). Cf. Karl Wolffsohn, *Jahrbuch der Filmindustrie* (Berlin: Verlag der Lichtbildbühne, 1930), vol. 4, 18, which reported already in November 1928 that Staaken had been absorbed by an English consortium.

34. See LAB 58/2676, vol. 1, 1–7.

35. Ibid., 15–19.

36. Subsequent to the charge against Zöhrer the Trade Commission cooperated briefly with George Pearson of International Talking Screen to replace Sklarz and Zöhrer and then abruptly withdrew its representatives from the company altogether. See 'Umgruppierung der Derussa', *Film-Kurier* (14 September 1929).

37. See 'Bericht über die bei der Derussa vorgenommene Prüfung' (11 November 1929) in LAB 58/2676, vol. 6.

38. This included reference to the disreputable past of the Sklarz family as a whole.

39. See the discussions in 'Vor und hinter den Derussa-Kulissen', *Lichtbildbühne* (21 September 1929), 11; 'Handelsvertretung und Derussa', ibid. (26 September 1929); 'Derussa und Handelsvertretung', *Film-Kurier* (19 September 1929); 'Offene Worte an Schwedschikow', ibid. (21 September 1929). For a general post-mortem with considerable insight into circumstances in the Soviet Union see Fritz Rosenfeld, 'Die Krise des Russenfilms', *Hamburger Echo* (26 October 1929).

40. See LAB 58/2676, vol. 2, 87–88.

41. The case file, which runs to 75 folios, consists largely of detailed examination of the charges raised by the first accountant.

42. While inquiries from the Ministry could be seen as routine, in this case they appear to have been motivated by the notoriety of Sklarz and the fear that right-wing sources would renew accusations that Sklarz was being shielded by Republican justice. See the memoranda in LAB 58/2676, vol. 5, 2,4,56,58.

43. The indictment is in ibid., vol. 3, 133–41.

44. See ibid., vol. 3, 213 & 219; vol. 4, 107–108, 127–35. In late 1933 Zöhrer refused to stand trial without Sklarz's participation, and Sklarz, though not a defendant, had his own good reasons not to

return: the Nazis had already exacted their revenge on his brother Heinrich – and on Weimar justice – by imposing a penitentiary sentence for events first tried in the mid-1920s.

45. The most famous case of crisis and American bailout was UFA's deal with Paramount and Metro-Goldwyn to form Parufamet in December 1925. See Thomas Saunders, 'Rettung in den Verlust: Die Parufamet-Verträge', in Hans-Michael Bock & Michael Töteberg, eds., *Das Ufa-Buch* (Frankfurt a.M.: Zweitausendeins, 1992), 174–79.

46. Sklarz admitted that favourable prospects lay behind the expansion of Derussa's payroll to over 100 employees. Whether this expansion, and the inflated salaries and allowances, can be described as criminal is quite another matter. See LAB 58/2676, vol. 2, 9.

47. Cf. the submission of the Trade Commission's lawyer of 3 October 1929 in ibid., vol. 1, 39–45; Zöhrer's lawyer cited much lower figures for a series of Derussa pictures, but admitted that at the time of Zöhrer's alleged fraud the three features in production had total projected costs of just over 400,000 marks, ibid., 67–74.

48. For details on this transaction, with the testimony of Pop and Sklarz, see ibid., vol. 48, 22–29. Cf. 'Sonderbericht über die Entstehung der Verlüste' in ibid., vol. 6, 4–7. The deal appears to have been Hermann Saklikower's cue for leaving the company.

49. Pop argued that the Phönix contract was Zöhrer's cause for extracting a pledge from Sklarz to abstain from interference in company management. See ibid., vol. 13, 2–5, for the agreements of September 1928 to keep Sklarz at arm's length from company policy. Sklarz denied this connection, claiming that his marginalisation was politically motivated.

50. The Richard-Hirschfeld Co. appealed in an open letter to the trustee overseeing bankruptcy proceedings for release of the names of those who had given loans at such exorbitant rates. See 'Offener Brief an den Konkursverwalter der Derussa', *Lichtbildbühne* (5 October 1929), 11.

51. LAB 58/2676, vol. 6, Anlage IV: 'Übersicht über Kosten, Leihmieten und Lizenzerträge der Derussa am 31 August 1929'. Cf. 'Wie es in der Derussa aussah', *Lichtbildbühne* (2 October 1929).

52. Most of this biography is from his submission to the court of 14 February 1931 in LAB 58/2676, vol. 3, 48–49. Cf. his earlier statements in ibid., vol. 1, 29–30.

53. See ibid., vol. 3, 49–51, for his claim of 30 million

marks sales for Sovkino. Cf. Denise Youngblood, *Movies for the Masses* (Cambridge: Cambridge University Press, 1992), 61, for the period 1921–28; 'Russisches Filmkontor in Deutschland', *Lichtbildbühne* (7 November 1928).

54. See LAB 58/2676, vol. 3, 49–51. Zöhrer referred contemptuously to the staff of the Trade Commission as civil servants interested only in balancing the books while he acted aggressively to maximise the sale of Soviet film abroad. This, combined with his reliance on Sklarz, helps explain his participation in purchase of the eight pictures from Phönix-Film.

55. Ibid., vol. 1, 59. Despite this Sklarz confirmed that Zöhrer succeeded in using Derussa as a springboard to make Soviet film popular abroad.

56. See Sklarz's lengthy written submission of 4 March 1930 in ibid., vol. 2, 4–12, here especially 4–7. Significantly, Sklarz set little store by sales to the Soviet Union where, although German pictures were widely distributed, they were commercially disadvantaged by the fact that prices were dictated by a state distribution monopoly rather than negotiated on a competitive market. Indeed, by 1927, as sales of Soviet motion pictures to Germany expanded rapidly, German distributors increasingly resented the arbitrariness and red-tape encountered with Soviet censors and the ridiculously low rental prices. On the monopoly and low prices see Kepley, 'The Origins of Soviet Cinema', 73. German frustrations were articulated in Josef Somlo, 'Filmrußland', *Lichtbildbühne* (2 April 1927): 10; 'Unangebrachte Vormundschaft', ibid. (10 September 1928); Lothar Stark, 'Film-Rußland und wir', ibid. (15 September 1928): 14–16. Derussa was caught in the middle, defending Soviet policy on the grounds that Russia bought German film stock and equipment and that most Russian cinemas could not be compared in size and profitability to their German counterparts. See the long press statement from Zöhrer in 'Rußland und wir', ibid. (26 September 1928).

57. This fact, combined with his formal removal from company operations in September 1928, became Sklarz's grounds for pleading ignorance, and innocence, of the transactions which brought disaster.

58. LAB 58/2676, vol. 2, 8–9. On European consortiums against Hollywood see Daniel Otto, '... Die Filmindustrie Europas retten! Wengeroff, Stinnes und das "Europäische Filmsyndikat"', in Schöning (ed.), *Fantaisies Russes*, 59–82. Sklarz's scheme resembled in principle the one Otto describes, so that Otto's claim (p. 76) that no serious efforts were made at such a consortium after the collapse of the Stinnes project in 1925 at least requires qualification.

59. In retrospect it is evident that his pan-European scheme, like the deal negotiated with International Talking Screen Productions, was also a desperate gambit to keep Derussa and Staaken afloat. Pop admitted to the court that Derussa was in trouble in late 1928 and would have declared bankruptcy in early 1929 but for the promise of English money. See LAB 58/2676, vol. 23, 2.

60. See his testimony of 4 March 1930 in ibid., vol. 2, 6–7. Sklarz argued that had Derussa contracted for import of political pictures it would never have agreed to a guarantee of US$7000 per picture, since American features could be purchased for roughly $2,000.

61. Ibid., vol. 1, 201.

62. Ibid., vol. 1, 58–59, 201. The closest the formal contracts came to such a definition was in a preamble: 'Sowkino und Staaken stellen gemeinsam und für gemeinschaftliche Rechnung Spielfilme zur kommerziellen Auswertung an allen Kinomärkten der Welt her'. Ibid., vol. 1, 181. Reference to 'feature films' and 'commercial exploitation' did not, however, unambiguously exclude what Sklarz would have labelled political propaganda.

63. Under close questioning they conceded that the social content of Soviet pictures could lead critics to identify political messages but denied that the term 'export film' had meaning in itself or relevance for Sovkino's offerings to Derussa. See ibid., vol. 7: minutes of arbitration hearing (19 December 1932), 12, 29–33.

64. Youngblood, *Soviet Cinema*, 112–113, 125, notes that Sovkino's production program for 1927 and 1928 projected big pictures which, while making concessions to political demands, were to be primarily apolitical.

65. A massive purge of foreign films in Soviet distribution and announcement in July of a production program for 1928–29 which would toe the Party line were the major inroads. Youngblood, *Soviet Cinema*, 162.

66. The transformation can be followed in Youngblood, *Soviet Cinema*, ch. 5–7 (a summary is in her *Movies for the Masses*, 28–32); Peter Kenez, *Cinema and Soviet Society 1917–53* (Cambridge: Cambridge University Press, 1992), ch. 5.

67. LAB 58/2676, vol. 7, (18 December 1932), 29, 44. Shvedchikov's lead was followed by an assistant, who claimed that the Soviets produced for their own market, unlike the Americans, and then exported what seemed appropriate. Ibid., vol. 7, 46–47.

68. Ibid., vol. 7, 26–27. Shvedchikov's assistant went further (p. 57), maintaining that the source of interest in the contract for Sklarz and Kaufmann was *Potemkin, The End of St Petersburg, Mother* and *Potomok Chingiz-khana* (Storm over Asia, 1928), not the so-called export films.

69. On both see Youngblood, *Movies for the Masses*, 84–87.

70. LAB 58/2676, vol. 6, Anlage IV: 'Übersicht über Kosten, Leihmieten und Lizenzerträge der Derussa am 31 August 1929'.

71. See the chapter on 'Genres and Hits' in Youngblood, *Movies for the Masses*, 71–89.

72. As late as spring 1929 Hans Pander noted that hardly any reviewers dared criticise Soviet imports. See his review of *Zuchthaus [Penal Servitude]* in *Der Bildwart* (April 1929), 227–8. Cf. Felix Gong, 'Die Welt ohne Grenzen', *Deutsche Republik* (21 September 1928), 1650, who referred critically to the snobbish tendency to greet everything Russian as an artistic revelation. Edmund Zöhrer fed the mystique in a radio lecture of July 1928 which presented Soviet cinema as 'something entirely new'. See 'Die Deutsch-russischen Filmbeziehungen', *Lichtbildbühne* (27 July 1928), Cf. Thompson, 'Eisenstein's Early Films Abroad', 59.

73. Pander's opinion is cited from *Der Bildwart* (April 1929), 228. For Schacht see his 'Russische Film, amerikanische und deutsche', *Der Kunstwart*, 40 (1927): 55–57. Cf. Gong, 'Begleitmusik', *Deutsche*

Republik (30 December 1927), 415. Georg Herzberg remarked that it was no easy task to stir the same political passions in the audience, year after year, but required an ongoing search for novel approaches. See his review of *Zuchthaus* [*Penal Servitude*] in *Film-Kurier* (1 February 1929).

74. Ernst Jäger, 'Das Ende von St Petersburg', *Film-Kurier* (27 February 1928). Cf. the review of *Zuchthaus* [*Penal Servitude*] in *Lichtbildbühne* (1 February 1929).

75. See Youngblood, *Soviet Cinema*, 206–207.

76. LAB 58/2676, vol. 2, 7.

77. See 'Verzerrt zur Grimasse', *Hamburger Echo* (14 September 1929). The Berlin voice of the German Communist Party showered praise on the film, confirming its political agenda. See Durus, 'Ein russischer Film der Kommune 1871', *Rote Fahne* (16 August 1929), reproduced in Kuhn et al. eds., *Film und revolutionäre Arbeiterbewegung*, 401–2.

78. Soviet imports did not subsequently appear in the list of most successful features at the box office polled by *Film-Kurier*.

79. See the chart in Youngblood, *Soviet Cinema*, 242, on the drastic drop in production from 1930 to 1932. For export complications and political obstacles to co-production see 'Brief aus Moskau: Film-Rußland und das Ausland', *Film-Kurier* (30 December 1929).

Film History, Volume 9, pp. 189–199, 1997. Copyright © John Libbey & Company
ISSN: 0892-2160. Printed in Australia

If truth be told, can 'toons tell it? Documentary and animation

Sybil DelGaudio

Whether one defines documentary as John Grierson's 'creative treatment of actuality',[1] or accepts Trinh T. Minh-ha's position that 'there is no such thing as documentary',[2] the term, always dynamic, has undergone continual scrutiny and re-consideration throughout film history.[3] From the infamous 'staged events' of Flaherty's *Nanook of the North* (1922), through the dramatisations of Errol Morris' *The Thin Blue Line* (1991), each new documentary has stretched the boundaries of preceding definitions, expanding potential beyond the confinement of the set criteria of contemporary theory.

In *Representing Reality*, Bill Nichols has suggested four modes of representation that 'stand out as the dominant organisational patterns around which most [documentary] texts are structured'.[4] Designating modes as expository, observational, interactive and reflexive, Nichols offers an approach that organises documentary into '[four] distinctive approaches to the representation of reality'.[5] The expository documentary (works by Flaherty and Grierson, for example), attempted to present information about the historical world and to see that world in a new way; observational documentary (Leacock, Wiseman, Pennebaker) arose as a reaction to the moralising quality of expository documentary and to the availability of more mobile and synchronous equipment which provided the opportunity to record events more unobtrusively;

interactive documentary (Rouch, de Antonio, Connie Field) arose from the desire to 'make the filmmaker's perspective more evident', while reflexive documentary (Vertov, Morris, etc.) arose from a desire to 'challenge the impression of reality which the other three modes normally conveyed unproblematically'. As the most 'self-aware' of the four modes, the reflexive mode utilises the devices of other documentaries, foregrounding such devices in an effort to emphasise them as well as the effects that they might achieve.[6] Reflexive documentaries such as Errol Morris' *The Thin Blue Line* and Dziga Vertov's *Man With A Movie Camera* (1929) constantly question the fabricated nature of the image as a mere function of the text itself. *The Thin Blue Line,* for example, frequently disrupts documentary practices as a means of conveying what Matthew Bernstein has termed its 'epistemological skepticism'.[7] The film re-enacts the crime from various perspectives to remind the viewer of 'what every filmmaker knows: that every representation, however fully imbued with documentary significance, remains a fabrication'.[8] Particularly interesting

Sybil DelGaudio is an associate professor at Hofstra University. Her current work-in-progress is a documentary on the lives and work of John and Faith Hubley. Correspondence: Department of Audio/Video/Film, 111 Hofstra Hall, Hofstra University, Hempstead, N.Y. 11550, USA Tel. (516) 463–5431.

about *The Thin Blue Line*, is that, while it re-creates several 'potential realities' in order to arrive at a theoretical truth (Randall Adams' innocence), the idea of an irrefutable truth is still elusive, since what Morris is really presenting in the film is speculative, however convincing it may ultimately be for some viewers.[9]

Further complicating the crisis of naming in documentary are animated films that deal with non-fiction subjects. Since an animated film 'exists' only when it is projected – there is no pre-existing reality, no pro-filmic event captured in its occurrence – its classification as documentary can be problematic. Without any existence in the world of actuality, the animated film must, like the partially dramatised documentary, rely on a kind of artistic re-enactment, depending, in part, on imaginative rendering of one sort or another[10] that may serve as compensation for the camera's non-presence at the event. Recent documentary theory, such as Brian Winston's idea that new technologies including digital manipulation have prompted interrogation of the ontological properties of the photographic image, while computer-based technologies such as the 'Harry' can manipulate the moving image in ways that are nearly completely undetectable;[11] or Philip Rosen's suggestion that cinema's reliance on 'not-able delay' (due primarily to the time it takes to 'process, manufacture and/or distribute the repre-senations') indicates a 'temporal disjunction' between the event and its perception by an audience,[12] demonstrate the continual questioning of both the mimetic nature of the photographic image and the reliance on its mimesis in the investigation of a film's classification as documentary. I will argue that such ongoing questions open the door for consideration of certain animated films as documentaries.

Animation history, which precedes live-action film history through the technology of optical toys,[13] presents many examples of works that deal with 'actuality' by using animation to re-tell a story. Winsor McCay's *The Sinking of the Lusitania* (1918) 'documented' the infamous event of the 1915 sinking of the British passenger ship by a German U-boat. The film, which represented McCay's own outrage, as well as a depiction of the event that had been widely represented in editorial cartoons of the period, was painstakingly rendered over the course of 22 months, in 25,000 drawings on clear cels.[14] The film's animation technique, because of its resemblance to live-action in some sequences and its stylistic reliance on editorial cartooning in others,[15] presents a passionate and journalistically convincing re-telling of an event that had never been photographed.

Max and Dave Fleischer[16] continued in the tradition created by McCay with two films based on scientific theories. In both *Evolution* (1925) and *The Einstein Theory of Relativity* (1923), Max Fleischer utilised techniques of combining live-action with animation as well as with still photographs and other illustrative materials, to explore and support the credibility of Darwin's and Einstein's work. Released at the time of the Scopes trial, *Evolution* provoked the wrath of fundamentalists who objected to a Darwinian view of creation.[17] Later in the century, as World War II enlisted the cooperation of many large corporations in the war effort, Disney made *Victory Through Air Power* (1943), a feature-length animated film based on Major Alexander P. de Seversky's book asserting the superiority of aeroplanes over more traditional armed forces which relied on tanks and ships, and calling for the creation of an air force as an independent branch of military service.[18] Critics had mixed reactions to the film, which combined a limited style of animation with Fleischer's earlier techniques of using stills and charts, but their responses, whether negative or positive, indicated its heavily propagandistic approach to the subject.[19] Following the war, and in an effort to maintain solvency for his studio, which was heavily in debt, Disney made many industrial and educational films for various corporations, including Dow Chemical, Texaco and General Motors, but his realisation of their limited commercial appeal discouraged him from continuing such projects, and except for a few that he considered good public relations for the studio (*How To Catch A Cold* in 1951, and *Our Friend the Atom* in 1957 are two examples), he ceased production of non-commercial films.[20]

Our Friend the Atom (1957) uses the metaphor of a fisherman who casts his net and snags a small jar containing a genie who promises to grant him three wishes. The fisherman's desire to master the mighty giant that will ultimately do his bidding is likened to humankind's desire to harness the power-

1156-84

Fig. 1. The genie of the atom comes to grant humanity three wishes in Disney's animated industrial film, *Our Friend the Atom* (©Walt Disney Productions, 1957).

ful force of atomic energy after having discovered the tiny atom that has imprisoned that force. The film goes on to identify humanity's three wishes for the use of atomic energy: power (the use of atomic energy to replace the dwindling coal and oil resources of our planet); food and health (the use of radioisotopes in medicine); and peace (the wise use of atomic energy for creation – not destruction).[21]

Carrying on the tradition of Disney corporate educational animated films, was the *Bell Science Series*, produced by Jack Warner for Bell Telephone. With several of the episodes written and directed by Frank Capra, and animation direction by such notable artists as Chuck Jones, Friz Freleng and Shamus Culhane, the series attempted to 'explain' scientific phenomena such as the nature of time (*About Time,* (1959)), the functioning of the human body (*Hemo the Magnificent,* 1958), the

importance of heredity and environment in determining human traits (*The Thread of Life,* (1957), and the mysteries of the universe (*The Strange Case of Cosmic Rays,* 1957), among others.[22]

Animated films proved a popular educational tool with adults as well as with children, and during World War II the government looked to animators for a more entertaining approach to training. The 18th Air Force Base Unit (also known as the First Motion Picture Unit) made animated films for the armed services, on subjects ranging from how to successfully utilise camouflage as a way of thwarting 'the enemy', (*Camouflage,* 1943) to how to shoot down an enemy plane (*Position Firing,* 1943).

Begun in 1942 by Rudy Ising, the First Motion Picture Unit (FMPU) was made up of approximately 80–100 enlisted men, officers and civil servants whose assignment was to make amusing and engaging training films for servicemen. Organised into four units headed by ex-Disneyites Frank Thomas, Berny Wolf, Van Kaufman and Joe Smith, 'FUM-POOH', as it was known by the men who worked there, produced hundreds of animated training films for various branches of the armed services.[23]

Because of its location in the old Hal Roach Studio in Culver City, the FMPU was also known as 'the Fort Roach Resistance' or 'the Culver City Commandos', a unit which produced films that were far more successful in appealing to trainees, who watched them 'more attentively' than they did live-action films or illustrated lectures. During the war, Fort Roach turned out more animation than any studio in Hollywood.[24]

Among the best-remembered films produced at Fort Roach were those made by Frank Thomas' unit, which starred a character named 'Trigger Joe'. *Position Firing,* the best known of the series, basically taught an important principle for shooting at enemy planes with greater accuracy (i.e. gunners needed to remember to take aim based not on where the enemy plane was, but on where it would be when the shot arrived). According to animator Bill Hurtz, the character was rooted in Hollywood war-film stereotypes, closely resembling the somewhat good-natured, but a bit slow-on-the-uptake roles played by actor William Bendix.[25]

Camouflage, a film made by the Thomas unit in which Hubley worked, presents a character not unlike Trigger Joe in design, and only slightly more intelligent than Joe in dealing with the challenges of war. Like many of the characters in these animated training films, 'Dodo', as he is called, needs to be educated. Beginning with a Disney-like introduction to the meaning and importance of camouflage in the animal kingdom, *Camouflage* presents several anthropomorphic animal characters (a butterfly, a bird, and a deer looking remarkably like Bambi) whose whereabouts are protected from their 'enemies' by their capacity to blend into their natural surroundings. We are soon introduced to Yehudi the Chameleon, another Disney-like character, who, by virtue of his own natural gifts, becomes the voice of authority on 'camouflage'.

Often during the war, the men of the First Motion Picture Unit moonlighted at United Film Productions, an early incarnation of what was later to become United Productions of America, or UPA. [26] In its early years, United Film Productions' work was frequently commissioned by government agencies (e.g. the State Department, Office of War Information Overseas Branch, and various branches of the armed forces, including Capra's army unit). For the Navy, United Film Productions did a series of films entitled 'Flight Safety', many of which were worked on or supervised by ex-Disney artist, John Hubley.[27] Among those surviving is *Flathatting* (1945), a black and white animated film describing the potential perils of flying too low, including showing off, hotdogging, etc., and illustrating the flatter, more stylised graphic approach that would later develop into UPA style.[28] In addition, the film delves interestingly into the psychological history of the hotdogging pilot, in an effort to understand his emotional makeup and motivation for doing what he does in the air, as well as to present the results and dangers of his unfortunate choices.

If we agree that 'representing reality', in Nichols' words, is of critical importance to the projects of certain animated films, I will argue that the reflexive mode seems a particularly appropriate mode in which to situate certain animated films, since animation itself acts as a form of 'metacommentary' [29] within a documentary, a form that is traditionally and most frequently characterised by live-action and non-dramatisation, particularly in the case of films which 'document the undocumentable', either because a camera has not been present at the event, or because the event has occurred at a time prior to photography or any other type of recording.[30]

In the 'theoretical' documentary, i.e. documentaries which explore and investigate theory, animation prompts the viewer to a 'heightened consciousness of his or her relation to the text and of the text's problematic relation to that which it represents'.[31] Even more specifically, in the case of films which explore or communicate principles of *scientific* theory (films such as *A Brief History of Time* (1992), by Errol Morris, an essentially live-action film that contains several animated images, or *Of Stars and Men* (1964), by John and Faith Hubley, a film that is entirely animated), animation serves to create a rupture between the signifier and the signified, thus reinforcing the theoretical nature of the information presented, and foregrounding the

Fig. 2. In such fully animated documentaries as *Of Stars and Men* (John and Faith Hubley, 1964), animation works to heighten the consciousness of the viewer's relation to the text.

aforementioned 'heightened consciousness' about its 'factuality'. Since scientific theory often walks a thin line between that which is knowable or provable, and that which is not, the reflexive mode emphasises the epistemological doubt inherent in the presentation of scientific theory through the medium of film, directly questioning knowledge by placing it in 'relation ... to issues about the ... difficulties of verification and the status of empirical evidence ... '[32] Recently, as Nichols further points out, events such as the Rodney King tapes have suggested that the status of the photographic image's 'ontological or evidentiary nature' is far from 'cut and dried', most notably in legal proceedings,[33] and perhaps has contributed, in part, to the degree to which subjective elements such as simulation have become an accepted part of documentary representation. As the viewer becomes more aware of the 'constructed image', questions about the adequacy of representation arise. As Nichols has queried, how can a filmmaker represent 'that

which is not readily available for documentation, having occurred in the past, out of sight of any camera?'[34] In the case of films that posit scientific theories, especially those that deal with such issues as the nature of time (*A Brief History of Time*) or the formation of the universe (*Of Stars and Men*), 'documenting the undocumentable' becomes both a practical and a philosophical concern, directly challenging myths, not only about the 'knowability' of the world,[35] but also about cinema's capacity to represent it.

In Errol Morris' *A Brief History of Time*, an investigation into the mind and theories of scientist Stephen Hawking, Morris consistently interrupts the presentation of scientific theory with images (often computer-generated, animated images) that highlight its epistemological nature while they simultaneously question cinema's ability to represent the world of scientific theory. Morris' unwillingness to assist Hawkings in the verification of the scientist's theories is evident in his presentation of material in a medium whose verifying capabilities he constantly questions. Since the filmmaker cannot hope to compete intellectually with the scientist's wealth of knowledge about a particular scientific subject, his skepticism is located in artistic 'metacommentary', speaking to viewers less about the world of scientific theory itself (a subject he knows little about in comparison to the scientist), than about the process of representation of that world. As an example of the reflexive mode of documentary, *A Brief History of Time* constantly 'emphasises epistemological doubt [by stressing] the deformative intervention of the cinematic apparatus in the process of representation'.[36]

While certain animation styles (i.e. Disney hyper-realism) seem concerned with the re-creation of reality, others, such as the style pioneered by UPA and later developed by John and Faith Hubley, are less so.[37] Hubley style, an outgrowth of the earlier UPA style, is, in fact, a direct response to Disney hyper-realism, an attempt to reveal, rather than conceal, that images are drawn. With its emphasis on contemporary graphics and social content Hubley style was less concerned with representational issues such as three-dimensionality and rotoscoping than was Disney . In this regard, it seems interesting to note that John Hubley, who worked on both the Disney version of the creation of the world (i.e. the 'Rite of Spring' sequence from *Fantasia* (1940)) and on the Hubley version of the same event in *Of Stars and Men*, was in the position of being able to re-evaluate an animated documentary's approach to theories about the same event using very different styles of animation.

In speaking about the *Rite of Spring* sequence, Hubley, who was the art director for three of the segment's eight sections (i.e. *Trip Through Space/Volcanoes/ Earthquakes*), explained what Disney had in mind: 'From the outset, *Fantasia* was conceived as a scientific document.'[38] John Culhane reports that 'Walt explained what he wanted in fifteen simple words: "As though the studio had sent an expedition back to the earth six million years ago"'.[39] Some of the volcanic activity was rotoscoped. Josh Meador, animation special effects supervisor, made vats of an oatmeal, mud and coffee mixture, bubbling it up with air hoses.

The action was filmed with high speed cameras, while individual frames were processed on cels dyed red against a yellow background. Animation was added to create more splashes and broaden the action.'[40] Further attesting to its 'realism' is a statement by documentary filmmaker, Pare Lorentz, who reviewed the film in *McCall's* calling the sequence 'the most extraordinary motion picture I've ever seen on screen: it is by far the most daring, powerful, exciting and successful portion of *Fantasia*.[41]

In quite a different approach in *Of Stars and Men*, the Hubleys attempted to visualise Harlow Shapley's scientific theories about the cosmos, examining its four basic entities or properties: space, time, matter and energy. The 53-minute film, based on Shapley's book of the same title, opened at the Beekman Theater in New York on 29 April 1964 to uniformly excellent reviews. In their publicity material, the Hubleys described their style as 'animage', defined as 'graphic arts in motion'. Writing about it years later in *Film News*, John Canemaker said it 'does what PBS' *Cosmos* does, but with economy, directness and without the didactic Carl Sagan'. Narrated by Shapley himself, the film looks at 'what man is and where he is in the universe of atoms, protoplasm, stars and galaxies'.[42]

According to Faith Hubley, the project grew out of a desire John had had to do a film on Einstein's theory of relativity. Their difficulties in dealing with the Einstein estate proved to be insurmountable, and when Sidney Lumet suggested they read Shapley's book (at the time, Faith was working with him on *12 Angry Men*, (1957)), their interest in Shapley's views was peaked.[43]

Shapley had begun his career as an astronomer at the Mt. Wilson Observatory in Pasadena, and from 1921–52, served as the director of the Harvard College Observatory. He was the author of half a dozen books and hundreds of scientific articles, also having made several important contributions to the field of astronomy, including the measurement of the diameter of the Milky Way as a galaxy, the discovery that the centre of the galaxy is 25,000 light years away from the earth in the direction of Sagittarius, thus showing the eccentric position of the Earth and Sun in the stellar universe.

Fig. 3. In a search for added realism, volcanic activity in Disney's *Fantasia* (©Walt Disney Productions, 1940) was partially rotoscoped over images of bubbling oatmeal.

According to George Ellery Hale, the noted astronomer whose efforts resulted in the 100-inch telescope on Mt Wilson, Shapley was one of the 'most daring of the younger scientists ... much more venturesome than other members of our staff and more willing to base far-reaching conclusions on rather slender data'. According to science historian Anthony Serafini, this was indeed a compliment, since 'good science requires *some* risk taking and speculative theorising as well'.[44] Most importantly, 'his determinations proved that our solar system was not the "centre of the universe" as earlier astronomers

had believed, and that "in reality, we were negligently placed somewhere on the outskirts of our galaxy"'.[45]

In addition to their attraction to Shapley's scientific theories, the Hubleys were also morally, politically and philosophically in tune with the astronomer. Respected while he was at Harvard, Shapley became an outcast once he began talking about his philosophy of life and his politics.[46] His *New York Times* obituary, which refers to him as 'the dean of American astronomers', states that his entry into battles against ultranationalism, greed,

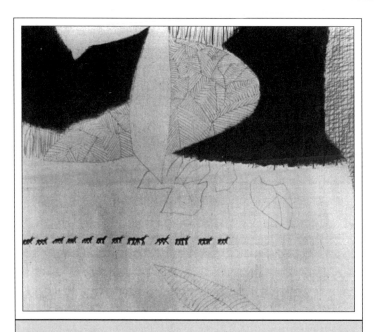

Fig. 4. While playing the festival circuit in the mid-1960s, the fully animated *Of Stars and Men* sometimes competed with live action films, sometimes with documentaries.

according to Faith, 'attacked a lot'. Richard Leacock 'hated it', while Kevin Smith was 'more sympathetic'. Submitted to the Venice Film Festival, it was placed in the feature category with live action films, while at the San Francisco Film Festival it won the documentary prize.[49]

In *Of Stars and Men*, Shapley's voice-over narration serves as the 'representative reality', ostensibly the voice of authority, which is, instead, consistently interrogated by the use of animation as 'metacommentary'. In terms of the way in which it approaches questions of cinematic representation, *Of Stars and Men* resembles Errol Morris' *A Brief History of Time* more closely than it resembles the 'Rite of Spring' sequence from *Fantasia*. With its stylised interviews, Morris' film 'blurs divisions between documentary and feature filmmaking by conducting all the interviews on elaborate studio sets', and using computer generated imagery to relate objects from everyday life (i.e. dice, teacups) to scientific concepts.[50] Morris describes the enterprise as similar to that which he used in *The Thin Blue Line*, i.e. 'an investigation into the nature of truth'.[51]

hunger, pride and prejudice; his support of a policy of coexistence rather than cold war in the late 1940s, and his efforts in the fight against what he termed the 'Red hunters' of the 1940s and 1950s, while his most significant contributions outside of astronomy, made him a figure subject to criticism and abuse, and ultimately brought him to confrontation with HUAC and Senator Joseph McCarthy.[47] In speaking about the film today, Faith Hubley says:

> It's a visionary documentary. How can you do a documentary about life on other planets? – you have to imagine it. It's about time, space, matter and energy. It's a way to put things into bite-size relationships. There's what we know; what we forgot; and what we can imagine. It's not a documentary in the strict sense, but it is a documentary in that it records what our place in those four basic entities has been, will be, etc. It shows us how to take joy in just being a player in that universe – it's glorious … Harlow Shapley, in my view, taught us genuine humility.[48]

Shown at a conference at MIT's Visual Department when it was finished, *Of Stars and Men* was,

In several ways, *Of Stars and Men* seems almost a direct reaction to the Disney approach used in *Fantasia* to tell a similar story. As a reflexive documentary, *Of Stars and Men* confronts issues of indexicality, not only by using animation, but by using a style of animation that directly challenges Disney realism. In its constant foregrounding of process, Hubley animation questions not only the ability of cinema to communicate 'truth', but, more specifically, the ability of animation to represent reality, a question that contributed, in part, to the 'graphic revolution' in animation begun by Hubley and other ex-Disney artists at UPA. The question of whether documentary should or must 'capture' reality is raised implicitly by *Of Stars and Men's* meditation on the issue of cinematic representation of the historical world.

Clearly this article has not considered *all* animated documentaries, nor has it approached the crisis of naming in as comprehensive a way as the question deserves. Issues such as the placement of Norman McLaren's *Neighbours* (1952) and Saul Bass' *Why Man Creates* (1970) in the documentary short subject categories of the Academy Awards might be interesting to investigate, as are more recent animated 'documentaries' by Aardman Animation, such as *War Story* (1989) and *Going Equipped* (1989), but these are subjects for further research. I have focused here on the reflexive documentary, highlighting two films that use animation to deal with scientific theory, and attempting to suggest that such films serve as a means by which a filmmaker can question the adequacy of representation in relationship to that which it represents, ultimately re-emphasising what 'every filmmaker knows: that every representation, however fully imbued with documentary significance, remains a fabrication'.[52] ♣

Notes

1. John Grierson, quoted in Paul Rotha, in collaboration with Sinclair Road and Richard Griffith, *Documentary Film* (New York: Hastings House, 1970), 70.

2. Trinh T. Minh-ha, 'The Totalizing Quest of Meaning', in *Theorizing Documentary,* ed., Michael Renov (New York: Routledge, 1993), 90.

3. As recently as 1995, Miramax Films, in response to what it perceived as the Motion Picture Academy's egregious neglect of recent 'documentaries' from the list of nominated films in that category, called for the alteration of the name of the category, from Best Feature Documentary, to Best Non-Fiction Feature, charging that the term 'documentary' had too many specifications that required veteran Academy members to eliminate from consideration certain films that did not conform to dated concepts of what documentary had been or could be. Works such as *The Thin Blue Line,* with its numerous dramatisations, or *Brother's Keeper,* with its carefully organised dramatic structure, have been noticeably absent from lists of nominated films in recent years, leaving the impression that the suspected backlash against successful theatrically released documentaries, is more accurately a matter of the crisis of naming than it is an angry punishment aimed at films that have had too much commercial success.

4. Bill Nichols, *Representing Reality* (Bloomington: Indiana University Press, 1991), 32.

5. Ibid., 32.

6. Ibid., 35.

7. Matthew Bernstein, 'Roger and Me: Documentaphobia and Mixed Modes', *Journal of Film and Video,* vol. 46, no. 1 (Spring, 1994): 4.

8. Nichols, 57.

9. As 'inconclusive' as Nichols suggests that Morris' evidence ultimately is, it seems ironic that the film itself became the impetus for Randall Adams' release from prison after twelve years. Here was a situation in which the film itself had a significant impact on the actual case, thus suggesting that Morris' argument was accepted – at least by those whose opionion held some weight – as 'truth'.

10. Animation, often defined as a film created one frame at a time, may be drawn or painted on cels or various kinds of paper, but there are other alternatives to drawn animation, among them stop-motion (using puppets, models, clay figures, etc.) and the more recent computer animation. 'Camera-less animation', i.e. animation created by drawing or painting directly on film, does not rely at all on the process of recording an image with a camera.

11. Brian Winston, 'The Documentary Film As Scientific Inscription', in Michael Renov, ed., *Theorizing Documentary* (New York: Routledge, 1993), 55–6.

12. Philip Rosen, 'Document and Documentary: On the Persistence of Historical Concepts', in Michael Renov, ed., *Theorizing Documentary* (New York: Routledge, 1993), 60.

13. As Richard Leskosky has reported, optical toys were 'full-fledged animation devices [which] created the illusion of motion through the presentation of a rapid succession of individual sequential images to the eye'. ('Phenakistoscope: 19th Century Science Turned to Animation', *Film History,* vol. 5, no. 2 (1993), 176).

14. Charles Solomon, *Enchanted Drawings* (New York: Alfred A. Knopf, 1989), 18.

15. Donald Crafton, *Before Mickey* (Cambridge: MIT Press, 1984) 116. Crafton reports that the film's 'documentary' nature required a 'more realistic graphic style', and it seemed appropriate to utilise some of the characteristic crosshatching, washes and spatter techniques of the Hearst newspapers, both in terms of its expression of the artist's point of view and in its journalistic style of rendering). Crafton also reports that J.R. Bray, an animator who worked in the early teens, discovered an untapped

arena for animated films when he was commissioned by the United States Government to make army training films for soldiers. By 1919, Bray's instructional films were being ordered from private industry as well as from government sources, and even prompted a re-organisation of his studio's priorities to cover the demand (157–8).

(I am indebted to Mark Langer for his suggestion to contextualise John and Faith Hubley's *Of Stars and Men*, a film I discuss later, within the context of other animated 'documentaries' that have appeared throughout the history of film).

16. Max and Dave Fleischer, who opened their own animation studio in 1921, made odd and original films, using memorable characters such as Betty Boop and Popeye in mostly short works that provided a stylistic alternative to Disney hyper-realism. Fleischer animation was characterised by a more fluid, rubbery style than Disney's precise and heavily researched approach.

17. Solomon, 32.

18. Ibid., 126.

19. Ibid., 126–7. Solomon quotes Thomas Pryor, whose review in the *New York Times* referred to the film's 'inspiring propaganda', while James Agee's response in the *Nation* expressed his hope that Disney and de Seversky knew 'what they were talking about', since the public would undoubtedly be swayed by their powerful but one-sided argument. Both reviews deal with the film as a purveyor of 'truth', however subjective, never seeming to object to its use of animation to convey point of view.

20. Ibid., 183

21. Disney's homespun approach to atomic energy as our 'friend' differs markedly from the view of nuclear energy communicated by animation filmmakers, John and Faith Hubley, in their 1963 film, *The Hole* (1963). In this film, two demolition workers have a discussion on the frightening potential of nuclear war. The Academy-Award winning film, with voices and improvised dialogue by George Mathews and Dizzy Gillespie, stands as a challenge, not only to the supporters of the 'useful' nature of atomic energy, but also to Disney's naive acceptance of the idea that world powers will use the atom only in the wisest ways.

22. *The Whole Toon Catalog*, (Chicago: Facets Multimedia, 1996), 14. This made-for-television series is an interesting forerunner to John and Faith Hubley's *Of Stars and Men* (1961), an animated documentary based on scientific theory dealt with in greater detail later in this article.

23. Solomon, 113.

24. Ibid., 113.

25. Interview with Bill Hurtz (6 April 1996).

26. UPA was an animation studio begun by Dave Hilberman, Steve Bosustow and Zack Schwartz in 1944. Many of its artists, among them John Hubley, were ex-Disneyites who had not been welcomed back after the divisive Disney Studio strike of 1941.

27. John Hubley, an active participant in the Disney Studio strike of 1941, served in the First Motion Picture Unit. Not welcomed back to the studio following the war, Hubley went to work for United Film Productions (later UPA), becoming one of the major innovators and leading proponents of UPA style.

28. Known for its innovative, some say 'revolutionary', graphics and unusual subject matter, UPA became the avant-garde of animation in the 1940s and 1950s, re-defining animation's potential to move beyond gag-driven stories and anthropomorphic characters.

29. Nichols, 56.

30. Joseph P. Ellis, the Ford Foundation Professor of American History at Mount Holyoke College and the author of *American Sphinx: the Character of Thomas Jefferson*, writes that when Ken Burns asked him to appear on camera in a documentary Burns was making on Jefferson, Ellis warned that Jefferson was not an appropriate subject for a documentary. 'You cannot make a documentary film about Thomas Jefferson ... because Jefferson predates the photograph ... [Burns' style] could not work for an eighteenth century subject'. While Burns ignored Ellis' warning, Ellis' concern about not providing photographs for the film expresses the popular notion of the importance of the reliance on some kind of ontological evidence for the confirmation of documentary 'truth'. Joseph Ellis, 'Whose Thomas Jefferson Is He Anyway?', the *New York Times* (16 February 1997), 16.

31. Nichols, 60.

32. Ibid., 61.

33. Ibid., 153.

34. Ibid., 57.

35. Ibid., 57.

36. Ibid., 61.

37. The Hubleys began their long and succesful venture into independent animation with *Adventures of An** in 1956. Sponsored by the Guggenheim Museum, the film looked at creativity and the way in which adulthood can often repress the childlike instincts

that permit us to enjoy and experience the world of life and beauty. *Adventures* was important in both its technique and its content, attempting to introduce nonobjective art to a wider audience and eliminating the inking and painting process in animation that had resulted in rigid drawings on clear cels. Throughout their collaboration and as they continued to experiment with style and subject matter, the Hubleys won numerous international awards, including three Oscars out of seven nominations. Following John's death in 1977, Faith's commitment to independent filmmaking has continued, and she has made approximately one film per year since then, struggling constantly with the difficulties of finding funding for projects that represent the purity of artistic expression with concern for commercial success clearly secondary. Her subjects have ranged from the Amazon rainforest (*Amazonia*, 1990), to child advocacy (*Step by Step*, 1978), to the nature of time (*Tall-Time Tales*, 1993), and her work is consistently inspired by her fascination with the art and mythology of other cultures, including native American astronomical myths (*Starlore*, 1983), Australian Aboriginal art (*Cloudland*, 1994) and Hawaiian mythology (*Rainbows of Hawaii*, 1995), to name just a few.

38. John Culhane, *Walt Disney's 'Fantasia'* (New York: Abrams, 1983), 120.

39. Ibid., 120.

40. Ibid., 121.

41. Pare Lorentz, quoted in Culhane, 126.

42. John Canemaker, 'Of Stars and Men' (review), *Film News* (Fall, 1980), 36.

43. Interview with Faith Hubley (10 September 1996). I am grateful to Faith Hubley for her cooperation in providing information, stills and support for this article.

   Of Stars and Men and other Hubley titles are available on video cassette in the collection 'Art and Jazz in Animation', through Lightyear Entertainment, New York.

44. Anthony Serafini, *Legends in Their Own Time: A Century of American Physical Scientists* (New York: Plenum Press, 1993), 106.

45. Ibid., 107.

46. Because of his liberal politics, John Hubley left UPA in the 1950s, was later blacklisted, and opened his own studio, Storyboard Productions, where he worked with a 'front man' in order to maintain his anonymity.

47. 'Harlow Shapley: Dean of American Astronomers', (obit.), the *New York Times* (21 October 1972), 36.

48. Interview with Faith Hubley (10 September 1996).

49. Ibid.

50. *The Making of A Brief History of Time*, a documentary by Errol Morris (jacket copy).

51. Ibid.

52. Nichols, 57.

Film History, Volume 9, pp. 200–218, 1997. Copyright © John Libbey & Company
ISSN: 0892-2160. Printed in Australia

Invisible footage: Industry on Parade and television historiography

Jason S. Mittell

Recent trends in cultural history have turned toward the notion of 'marginality' in order to correct past injustices of traditional historical practice. Critical historiography poses the writing of history as a practice which reproduces or resists dominant power relations, in part through choices as to what lies within the 'centre' of the historical focus and what either lies on the margins or is excluded altogether. Thus historians interested in critical history have looked to the margins and exclusions of traditional historical practice to rediscover and reclaim the people, places and things that have been ignored or swept under the rug by most studies. Through this process of historiographically recentring marginalised peoples (women, people of colour, working classes), places (the Third World, rural America), and practices (popular culture), many vital historiographical injustices have been addressed and partially corrected.

Despite the success and viability of recentring marginal objects of history in order to redress dominant power plays, this type of practice leads to an overly simplistic assumption: since histories of the subordinate are usually marginalised, that which is historically marginalised therefore must be subordinate. This notion proceeds from the assumption that the practice of traditional history is fostered by and imbued with dominant power relations and therefore the historiographical product of these practices mirrors the societal distribution of power. But just as

theories of pure reflection are generally viewed as simplistic and passé within media studies, this notion of historiographical reflection must be complicated and elaborated upon. The practice of critical historiography is much too vital politically to be saddled with such a rudimentary and inaccurate model. Thus within this paper I wish to complicate and nuance this model of historiographical marginalisation by examining a text which is politically, economically, and ideologically dominant, yet which has been historically marginalised and ignored: the 1950s public affairs television program, *Industry on Parade.*

I am not examining this forgotten program in order to correct injustices of previous historians or rebalance the power relations that caused this bit of television history to be marginalised; rather my purposes are primarily to examine the historiographical, archival, and institutional processes that have led to the marginalisation of this seemingly dominant text, and secondarily to explore what this recovered text might offer to cultural historians. The marginalisation of *Industry on Parade* has not been

Jason Mittell is a doctoral candidate in Communication Arts at the University of Wisconsin – Madison. His research focuses on media history and cultural theory. Correspondence, University of Wisconsin Department of Communication Arts, Vilas Hall, 821 University Avenue, Madison, Wisconsin 53706 Tel. (608) 246-3020.

due to counter-hegemonic content or subordinate practice embodied by the text. Instead, this case study points to the ways in which cultural history, especially media history, faces the daunting situation of having an innumerable amount of 'the past' to reckon with, as thousands of television programs, theatrical performances, musical recordings, advertising pieces, and motion pictures are produced and discarded into the trash bin of our collective memory each year. Determining which of these cultural practices are remembered, recycled, and recorded is a key part of the historian's job. By illuminating structural processes that delimit and determine what aspects of 'the past' are allowed to live on as 'history', this case study will illustrate some of these mechanisms for selecting history, arguing against a notion of 'historiographical Darwinism' in which only the fittest and most worthy cultural practices survive. This case study will point to the mechanisms of marginalisation in order to help recover and revivify those marginalised practices which truly are politically subordinate.

Industry on Parade **and television history**

Although this study is primarily historiographical, concerned more with the processes of how history is written than the stories of the past that are history's content, it is vital to examine the history of *Industry on Parade* alongside this historiographical exploration, retelling its story and uncovering its 'facts'. Only by examining what *Industry on Parade* was and how it functioned as part of 1950s American culture can we begin to understand some of the ways that broadcast historiography has performed its marginalisation of this dominant text. In retelling the story of this program, I will point toward avenues of further study and analysis which lead to insights concerning television and cultural history of this era. I will not travel far down these roads, as I wish to focus on what this case offers to historians interested in historiographical practice, not on the multitude of issues raised by the history of this text.

Industry on Parade was a 15-minute syndicated public affairs television program that aired nationally from 1950 to 1960.[1] The program, produced by the National Association of Manufacturers (NAM), presented short newsreel-style pieces showing the industrial processes of the United States, providing behind-the-scenes glimpses of 'the symbol of progress and hope for the majority of people', American industry.[2] While it was framed as a 'factual' and educational documentary, *Industry on Parade* was heavy on propaganda, pushing pro-industry, patriotic, and capitalist ideologies. Episodes were initially divided into three to five short pieces exploring a particular industry, company, entrepreneur, or manufacturing process. In addition, episodes generally included two short commercial-like segments introduced as 'And now a word from industry...'; these segments were the most overtly propagandic portions of the program, with a voice-over proclaiming the glory of American capitalistic industry over communism, warning of inflation, promoting voting and conservation, and singing the praises of industry's effects on society. In 1958 the program switched formats, with each episode focusing on one issue or type of industry, combining diverse footage of multiple companies and aspects of the topic; typical titles of these episodes are 'Looking at Glass!', 'Waste Not, Want Not!' (focusing on salvage and recycling), and 'Setting the Standard!' (examining the American standard of living). Although NAM proclaimed that this shift created more self-contained and integrated episodes, this move was also economically driven, as it enabled NAM to recycle footage from previous episodes and repackage it within a topical framework.

The production history of *Industry on Parade* remains quite sketchy. *Industry on Parade* was not NAM's first venture into the realm of media propaganda – the organisation produced a radio program in the late-1940s, *Your Business Reporter*, and had a thriving motion picture service exhibiting pro-industry films in clubs, schools, and workplaces.[3] NAM's radio and television director, Johnny Johnstone, is credited with the idea of creating a television program in 1950. He worked in collaboration with Frank McCall, an NBC News Department Manager, to develop a sample reel of the program in the autumn of 1950. NAM's board of directors approved production of the series and worked with NBC to produce an initial thirteen-week run. Viewed as successful by NAM and the local stations airing the program, NBC and NAM renewed their partnership for 1951 and thereafter.[4] Arthur Lodge, one of the NBC producers who worked on the program, left NBC during the mid-1950s and began producing *Industry on Parade* through his own production company, Arthur Lodge Productions, after NBC decided to cease producing non-network programming. Lodge continued producing *Industry on Parade* with Johnstone until the program ended its run in 1960.

The relationship between NBC and the syndicated *Industry on Parade* seems to be quite anomalous according to typical histories of early television. Although NBC did not air the program through its network, NAM made primary offers of local syndication to NBC-owned and operated stations and affiliates. Syndication of *Industry on Parade*, which was offered at no charge to stations, appears to have been quite successful, with 45 stations broadcasting the series as of the end of October 1950.[5] By 1957, the program aired on 270 United States stations and on 42 foreign stations in 33 countries around the world (with dubbed translations of the voice-over for these foreign markets).[6] Initial syndication targeted larger markets, ranging from New York City and Los Angeles to Greensboro, North Carolina and Huntington, West Virginia.[7] By the mid-1950s, the program was reaching the majority of television markets in the United States. For example, the Wisconsin edition of *TV Guide* from January 1956 indicates that the program was aired on WMTV Madison, WBAY Green Bay, and WSAU Wausau (reaching the Milwaukee area), covering the State's three primary markets.[8]

As is the nature of syndicated programming, broadcast dates and times are determined by local markets. Thus *Industry on Parade* aired in a variety of timeslots throughout the country. According to NAM schedules from December 1950, the program was broadcast in almost every conceivable non-prime timeslot: Saturday 12:30 p.m. (WNBT New York), Monday 6:45 p.m. (WBZ-TV Boston), Tuesday 10:45 a.m. (KSTP-TV St. Paul, MN), Sunday 10:30 p.m. (KEYL San Antonio), Friday 12:45 p.m. (WBAL-TV Baltimore).[9] As years passed and television schedules became more dominated by network fare, *Industry on Parade* took up more stable residence as a time filler for local programming on weekend afternoons. While many programs tend to be scheduled in conjunction with similar themed shows, *Industry on Parade* was partnered

with the full gamut of television genres. For example, it was sandwiched between *Oral Roberts'* religious services and *Warmap Theatre* on New York's WPIX in 1955.[10] In Wisconsin, it found the unlikely bedfellows of *Stagecoach Theatre* and *Grandma's Attic* (a children's program) on Madison's WMTV, while WBAY placed it between educational programs *Your Own Home* and *TV Hour* and WSAU programmed it following public affairs mainstay *Face the Nation* and preceding the anthology drama *Front Row Center*.[11] While we cannot recreate the unusual and varied programming strategies these local stations used to schedule *Industry on Parade*, we can contextualise these schedules. Within an era when stations were in need of local programming to fill gaps in their schedules, without libraries of reruns and network programs to plug these holes, a show like *Industry on Parade* was an economical and effective piece of filler for any place within a station's schedule.

Although ratings for syndicated programs from the 1950s are hard to uncover, some evidence suggests that the program had a decent following. NBC's Programming Schedules give ratings for WNBT as compiled by the American Research Bureau; for the week of 1–7 December 1950, *Industry on Parade* at 12:30 p.m. on Saturday received an 8.7 rating, the highest score for WNBT's Saturday daytime schedule. The following month, it received a very low 0.3 rating for the week of 7–13 January 1951.[12] This huge swing suggests both the tenuous accuracy of this rating system and the spotty viewership *Industry on Parade* received in this market. Other accounts suggest more solid successes for the program. According to a 1952 article, Oklahoma City ratings placed *Industry on Parade* in the top five among local programming and the Milwaukee market reported that NAM's program outrated *Meet the Press*, its programming neighbour.[13] Other signs of its success include the tremendous growth in syndicators from 1950 to 1957 as mentioned above, as well as *Industry on Parade*'s crowning moment, receiving the Peabody Award for National Public Service Programming in 1955. Aside from these sketchy clues, little is known about the reception of *Industry on Parade*, with no information as to who watched the program and how the audiences engaged and negotiated with these texts.[14]

Another interesting sidelight in the history of *Industry on Parade*'s exhibition is how NAM continued to use the footage and programming generated for its show after each episode's initial airing. As mentioned above, they recycled footage in the late-1950s, re-editing previously used and new segments together with a voice-over track thematically emphasising one key aspect of American industry. Additionally, NAM circulated episodes on film to schools and community groups. As early in the program's run as 1952, NAM was distributing the program to 24 metropolitan school systems.[15] One estimate suggests that in 1954, over 3.5 million students were viewing NAM-sponsored films, including *Industry on Parade* as well as non-television material.[16] The film copies of the footage that reside at the National Museum of American History (NMAH) Archives Center suggest that this practice continued and grew. According to postage marks and labels on the cardboard mailers containing the film reels, these programs were widely distributed nationwide to schools and community groups through the 1960s.

While the production, distribution and exhibition of *Industry on Parade* all point to interesting historical questions as suggested above, the texts of the program also open doors for historical analysis. Although it would be nearly impossible to examine the entire run of the program as a singular text, primarily due to the impracticality of viewing and discussing over 500 episodes and a ten-year run, we can note some tendencies and commonalities about the various episodes of *Industry on Parade*. Within this paper, I will focus on one episode (#18, initial airdate 6 February 1951) as a specific text; I believe this episode to be typical in terms of the issues and questions it raises both for historical analysis and for the modes of representation found within the series as a whole. This episode contains four main segments, 'Mrs America Serves Again!', 'King Cotton's Court!', 'Tower of Glass!' and 'Radiophone Keeps 'Em Rolling!', and two shorter 'And now a word from industry…' segments.[17] My examination of this particular episode does not attempt to provide a comprehensive understanding of the content, context, and significance of a television program, but rather serves as a brief sketch illustrating the various readings and interpretative strategies a historian might take in attempting to utilise *Industry on Parade* as a historical document. As such, my readings are purposely underdeveloped and incomplete, serving more as test runs for numerous analytical approaches than as full-fledged textual analyses.

All of the program's segments can serve dual functions for historians, providing evidence of 'the way things were' in American industry during the 1950s as well as evidence of public discourses around American industry at the time. Thus a segment such as 'Tower of Glass!' would offer historians visual evidence concerning the architecture and industrial design pioneered by the Johnson Wax building in Racine, Wisconsin, but it also provides historians a glimpse of the ways in which industrial buildings were publicly presented and discussed during this era.[18] It is important to consider these dual historical functions – though empiricist historians may focus on the former role while cultural historians look toward the latter, both functions are worthwhile historiographical uses of the texts and could serve to further our understanding of 1950s industry, television and culture.

The use of *Industry on Parade* as an historical source raises key issues concerning the role of a television text for historians. Keith Jenkins distinguishes between 'traces' and 'evidence', suggesting that traces of the past exist before the historian uncovers them, but that these traces become evidence when the historian activates them into historical discourse to support a specific argument or interpretation.[19] Thus we might envision a segment of *Industry on Parade* as a trace of the past, produced within and providing knowledge about a particular historical era. But, utilising the 'Tower of Glass!' segment as evidence to support a history of industrial design places this trace into a specific historical discourse and it turns it into a particular form of evidence. The same trace (the *Industry on Parade* segment) may be used to support a cultural history of the ways in which architecture has been represented within media, turning the segment into evidence of discourses on progress and technology. The trace of the past has not changed – the segment remains identical on film – but its historiographical uses have allowed two very different forms of evidence to emerge from the same program. This process is central to my examination of an episode of

Fig. 1. Cameraman Marcel Rebiere and his assistant Fred Montague filming the production of glass blocks for *Industry on Parade*. [From *American Cinematographer*, September 1955.]

Industry on Parade for the varied forms of evidence that may emerge from the same traces of the past.

All of the segments of this episode provide opportunities for historians to draw upon *Industry on Parade* to construct historical evidence. As mentioned above, 'Tower of Glass!' provides visual images of industrial design and architecture that may no longer be available. Like many other episodes of the program, this segment offers moving image documentation which is unavailable through most forms of primary source material. Shots portraying the developments of Johnson Wax's building give architectural historians the opportunity to see a building as the focus of motion picture footage and the chance to draw upon this footage as evidence of key developments in design. Similar types of evidence are available within this episode for other forms of industry and history: 'King Cotton's Court!' shows the mechanical and labour processes needed to refine and mass-produce cotton in the 1950s, while 'Radiophone Keeps 'Em Rolling!' focuses on the uses of telecommunication technol-

ogies to streamline operations on the Erie Railroad. Throughout the run of *Industry on Parade*, nearly every American industry was documented and featured, providing extensive visual and verbal traces of the 1950s for industrial and technological historians; these traces may be activated as evidence to answer the question 'How were things back then?' for a range of industries and areas of study.

While this use of *Industry on Parade* as evidence documenting industrial conditions during the 1950s is potentially quite valuable, I believe the historiographical worth of the program is primarily in its use for cultural historians examining discourses on American industry and life during this era. For while the visual evidence of 'how things were' is rewarding, *Industry on Parade* is anything but a 'pure' vision of the truth of the past (if such a thing could possibly exist) – this program was a specifically constructed piece of public relations for American industry to promote itself to the publics of the United States and the world. Although the cameras often captured how things were, they were obviously directed to film particular aspects of industry and ignore others – depictions of pollution, worker exploitation, managerial abuses, and labour strife do not make it into the edited newsreels distributed by NAM (nor would we expect them to). Thus we need to look at *Industry on Parade* as a document of how American industry wished to represent itself, refracting the discourses presented on film using the lens of pro-industry and American promotion. By foregrounding the conditions of production of these discourses (i.e. NAM's desire to serve itself and its goals over the need to present things the 'way they really are'), we can read this text as evidence of not the way things were, but of how NAM constructed things to be, and may simultaneously consider counter-readings for what was being excluded or marginalised within *Industry on Parade*'s construction.

Thus we may read 'Tower of Glass!' and 'Radiophone Keeps 'Em Rolling!' as parts of a narrative of progress, suggesting that leaders of industry are always moving forward to create better and more efficient forms of technology for industry. 'King Cotton's Court!' echoes this discourse, with its focus on factory efficiency and the glories of processed fabrics such as rayon, but the segment presents a facade of worker satisfaction and happiness atop this theme of technological progress, as workers are shown contentedly folding and processing fabric, ignoring historical instances of labour exploitation and horrifying working conditions within the textile industry. There is no surprise here that an admittedly pro-industry program would ignore labour tensions and efface inadequate working conditions, and we can presume that many viewers in the 1950s saw through this facade as management propaganda, but we must resist the nostalgic impulse to ignore the contextual framing of these messages in exchange for the tempting 'truth-value' of the filmed images of labour tranquility and worker satisfaction. As critical historians, we must read these segments for their exclusions, filling in the gaps that NAM's discourses overwrite by using contextualising historical accounts. Additionally, the 'message from industry' segments of the program serve as clear indications on how dominant American society, as represented by the interests of NAM, viewed issues in American politics and life, including messages of anti-Com-

munism, pro-consumption, anti-inflation, and the perfect society of success and progress as fostered by industry. By combining these texts with other historical works, we can unpack the contradictory discourses within *Industry on Parade* and uncover the political work that went into creating dominant discourses within the 1950s.

Examples as mentioned above represent clearly dominant discourses of the 1950s, but *Industry on Parade* is not always as clear-cut and simple. This is especially true concerning gender in the workplace. There are many issues raised in *Industry on Parade* that warrant further exploration of the contradictions and conflicts embodied in the text, but the examination of gender roles seems an especially fruitful example of this type of textual (and contextual) analysis, drawing both upon a rich text and a vital area of academic study in a number of disciplines, including media studies, social history and sociology. Thus my analysis of this episode's gender representations serves as an example of the type of historical reading that cultural historians might undertake to explore the competing discourses found within this program concerning other social issues and axes of power as well. *Industry on Parade* certainly warrants a detailed analysis of class representations, as differences between workers, management, and consumers are mostly erased and downplayed, replaying the American myths of equal opportunity and economic meritocracy; likewise, the show's homogenous representations of racial and ethnic identities under the rubric of American whiteness opens the door to examine both the construction of this 'non-ethnic' identity and the brief moments of rupture within this white veneer. But I have chosen to explore gender roles because of the surprising variety of positions available to both women and men throughout the run of the program. It was partly my interest in gender roles that led me to select episode 18 as my 'typical' text because of the provocative issues raised in its final segment.

Within the 'Mrs America Serves Again!' segment, we can see an illustration of overlapping and competing discourses surrounding working women in the postwar era that defies simple categorisation or typical generalisations about popular culture within this era. A segment such as this one calls attention to the internal contradictions of the notion of 'dominant culture' as a singular, uncomplicated position; *Industry on Parade* successfully presents contradictory messages which forces us to reconsider the strict duality between 'dominant' and 'marginal'. But before looking at how this segment represents gender and fits into its postwar historical context, we must consider some of the controversies and trends in historical work on this era, specifically concerning the central issue of gender roles in popular culture.

There are competing historical myths about the role of women in postwar America. Joanne Meyerowitz and Stephanie Coontz both work to dismantle one stereotypical conception of 1950s womanhood using the television figure of June Cleaver from *Leave it to Beaver*.[20] This mythic fiction suggests that no matter what strides women's labour took during World War II, women happily yielded their newly found place within the workforce to their returning husbands, took up residence in the suburban family ideal, and dedicated their lives to pleasing husband and children. Coontz suggests that this myth is often activated in order to fuel conservative attacks on feminism and 'alternative' models of family life, while Meyerowitz shows this stereotype as a mask that obscures more diverse and multiple histories of women's roles in the postwar era. But for both historians, television icon June Cleaver is the easily reducible symbol of this dominant conception of 1950s femininity. Within both of their revisionist historical accounts, television functions primarily as the site of rearticulation of this dominant ideal of domestic womanhood, as they ignore any competing or alternate representations of women on television during this era.

Meyerowitz and Coontz counter the June Cleaver model with historical accounts of women that do not fit into this ideal. Both Coontz, through her use of statistical accounts of women in the labour force, and Meyerowitz, by analyzing magazine discourses surrounding women's labour and family roles, show that women were indeed a growing part of the workforce during the 1950s and that this fact was not as hidden from the public eye as some feminist critical accounts might have suggested.[21] Meyerowitz's account effectively portrays the 1950s as an era in which women's roles were not uniform, homogenous or 'simple', and that popular culture reflected and participated in the multiplicity

of female representations and positions. Despite this, however, television remains the realm of culture that goes mostly unquestioned within their accounts. The June Cleaver figure prevails as a stand-in for television as a whole. Few analyses of postwar gender roles consider television as anything but a site of domination and domestic prescription.[22] But *Industry on Parade*, specifically in the 'Mrs America Serves Again!' segment, clearly demonstrates how televisual representations of women's roles in the 1950s, just like these roles themselves, were not as uniform, homogeneous or simple as many historians would seem to believe. As such, a close examination of gender roles within *Industry on Parade* works to displace the central assumption that televised women of the 1950s were wholly domesticated, subordinate and complacent.

'Mrs America Serves Again!' follows the career of an apparently typical female worker at Republic Aircraft on Long Island. This 'Mrs America' has followed a path that the narrator suggests is typical of American women of this era. During World War II, while her husband was abroad in the service, she helped her national cause by working for Republic, building the planes and weaponry that men like her husband used overseas. When the war ended and he returned to Long Island, she returned to the home to tend to her family while her husband went back to work. But as the years went by, she was 'called back into service' for her country, rehired by Republic to continue producing aircraft and weaponry for national defence. *Industry on Parade* frames this move as necessary for the United States to triumph over (unnamed) threats to national security, but running through this description is acknowledgement that it is financially helpful for both parents to be working while raising the seven children who are part of this 'typical' family. Additionally, NAM suggests that this 'woman's work' is rewarding not only to American defence but also to this female worker, a view that seems anathema to the discourses circulating years later on domestic sitcoms like *Leave it to Beaver*.

Industry on Parade argues that this story of 'Mrs America' is not atypical; the announcer proudly proclaims that 'constantly growing numbers of housewives and mothers' are working outside of the home. While NAM's statistics seem quite low,[23] the program clearly frames growing female employment as an unequivocally positive move that is necessary for industrial progress and national security. The episode even goes so far as to suggest total equality (and potential superiority) for women working in factories: the announcer proclaims, 'there isn't a part of even the most intricate instrument or weapon that American women can't produce as well as their menfolk… and in some cases, they do much better'. In other episodes, NAM clarifies in what cases women may be superior, offering that certain high-technology devices are better assembled by the 'small and delicate' hands of female workers. While there is none of this gender pandering in 'Mrs America Serves Again!', clearly this televisual representation is markedly different from the stereotypical view of women, typified by June Cleaver or *Father Knows Best* (especially in the widely considered 'Betty Wants to be an Engineer' episode).

Fig. 2. Producer Arthur Lodge, NAM public relations director G.W. 'Johnny' Johnstone, and film editor Roger Young inspect a sample reel of *Industry on Parade*. This photo appeared in an advertisement for Dupont Motion Picture Film in the September 1955 issue of *American Cinematographer*.

Not only does 'Mrs America Serves Again!' provide an example of supposedly non-dominant representations of women in the workplace, but the vision of the American family here is far from the alleged domestic ideal. The cameras follow 'Mrs America' to her home where we see how a working mother changes the domestic situation. Since her husband arrives home from work before she does, we see him starting to cook dinner. As the voice-over suggests, 'in a family where mother's a defence worker, everybody has to help out'. Thus we see father, mother, and all seven children (both boys and girls) equally pulling their weight in chores and dinner preparation. While this scene was obviously staged for NAM's cameras, this segment circulates a discourse in direct opposition to the 'typical' image of the 1950s suburban domestic ideal. If June Cleaver stands in for a representation of the ideal

mother and wife, 'Mrs America' serves as a counter-representation of a more egalitarian and balanced domestic situation which preceded the Cleavers on television by over five years.

While I have examined 'Mrs America Serves Again!' as a vital text for understanding the complexities and heterogeneity of discourses surrounding gender in the 1950s, I should note that this segment serves as an extreme but not atypical example of *Industry on Parade*'s representations of women in the workplace. Throughout the run of the series, women were featured prominently as factory workers, business owners, stockbrokers, entrepreneurs, secretaries and inventors. Similarly, women were often in the background of the frame as the staff of the industries visited by NAM's cameras. Thus although no other segment appears to be as 'radical' as 'Mrs America Serves Again!', this segment was not a 'token' examination of working women while all other episodes focused on men. I do not wish to overstate this claim, as certainly the bulk of *Industry on Parade* footage shows American men working and using the fruits of their labour, but I believe that a program such as this can go far to dispel the notion that the *only* televisual representations of women in the 1950s were as housewives and mothers. As such, historians must look to many programs of this era, including non-fiction shows like *Industry on Parade* as well as fictional representations of women in the workplace such as *Private Secretary*, before making generalisations about television as the domain of exclusively domestic female characters in the 1950s.[24]

Industry on Parade and television historiography

If *Industry on Parade* presents such a rich and interesting case study of multiple aspects of television history, exemplifying issues of varied institutional methods of production, distribution and exhibition, as well as offering key entries into our history of industrial development and gender representations, how has the program been remembered by television historians? Surveying the growing literature on broadcasting history, it appears that the program has been completely ignored. None of the television histories of this era that I examined even mention *Industry on Parade*.[25] In this section, I will attempt to account for this lack of historical acknowledgement and point to specific factors that may have contributed to the shaping of visual history to exclude this remnant of the past. In doing so, I will point to some larger gaps in broadcast histories that contribute to *Industry on Parade*'s erasure, including lacks of focus on syndication, 15-minute programming, public affairs programs, and programming itself. Additionally, I will consider some of the historiographical limitations and possibilities that are delimited by the NMAH archival storage practices by exploring my own experience as an archivist working on *Industry on Parade*. Finally I will consider how *Industry on Parade* can serve as an example of greater issues of historiography and marginalisation within television history.

Any attempt to coherently survey 'broadcast history' is obviously fraught with peril; just as the study of media is scattered across disciplines and methodologies, the histories of media are varied in approach and scope. A particular history might focus on policy issues, technological developments, industrial structures, programming content, or a specific question or gap raised by previous historians. I do not claim to be comprehensive in my survey of broadcast histories for accounts of *Industry on Parade* and patterns of historiography that have led to the program's historical erasure. Instead I have looked at what I believe to be some typical histories that may shed light on these issues. In doing so, I have divided my choices of broadcast histories into two main categories: 'comprehensive' narratives and selective investigations.

The 'comprehensive' narrative is typical of the history textbook. It attempts to tell a chronological story of the emergence of broadcasting as we now know it, touching on all areas of interest along the way, including policy, technology, programming and industry. I have left the term 'comprehensive' in quotation marks for obvious reasons: no history can be truly complete in scope and accuracy, especially when covering a multiplicitous topic such as broadcasting. Yet the implication of these 'comprehensive' texts is that, while they are not exact replications of the past, they do capture the key details and events that inform their readers of 'what happened' in terms of broadcasting's emergence and development. There are no self-reflexive caveats or statements of specific theses in these texts; instead, the authors of a 'comprehensive' narrative history have attempted to retell the story of the past in a way that attempts to recreate it, consistent with Jenkins' notion of empiricist history which uses traces of the past as evidence of the 'truth' that actually happened.

The two main texts that I have included under this category of 'comprehensive' narrative are *Stay Tuned* by Christopher Sterling and John Kittross, and Erik Barnouw's multi-volume *History of Broadcasting in the United States*.[26] These authors preface their histories with statements of purpose that typify this historiographical approach. Sterling and Kittross write, 'we have tried to note the important events and themes in American broadcasting's story through careful selection of items to include in this single volume and subjects to analyze at length'.[27] While they seem to acknowledge that their Herculean task of telling the entire story of broadcast history in one volume is quite difficult, they suggest that through wise selection and research they can in fact accomplish their goal. Explicit in their preface is the notion that through proper dissemination of historical facts, the past may be fully comprehended. Likewise Barnouw is vested in retelling the full story of the past; he suggests that he 'will examine what was broadcast, by whom, and why'.[28] Barnouw admits that the 'why' question is most daunting as it requires examination and interpretation of the 'behind-the-scenes' stories, but he accepts this challenge and attempts to portray these complex reasons as facts throughout his texts. The key motivation behind both of these histories is the desire to narrativise and disseminate the past as history without any particular thesis or argument framing the narrative.

Given the monumental goals set forth by these authors, it is not a surprise that their histories are full of omissions, gaps, oversimplifications, and inaccuracies. But it does seem surprising that *Industry on Parade* and similar programs are completely omitted from these grand narratives. This is partially due to emphasis of topic – Sterling and Kittross foreground technological and industrial developments over programming issues, while Barnouw emphasises specific case stories often focusing on the relationship between broadcasting and politics. Yet this is not a full explanation, for *Industry on Parade*, as I suggested above, provides an interesting case concerning issues of both industry and politics, one that complements and contradicts the views put forth in these texts. There are other prioritisations and marginalisations within these texts that can help account for *Industry on Parade*'s absence.

Sterling and Kittross do not just background programming content and specific shows in favour of industrial structures; they also ignore certain key aspects of the television industry. They assert the dominance of network programming early and often, only mentioning syndication in passing as cheap filler for non-prime-time schedules. Within *Stay Tuned*, non-network programming remains an 'other', occasionally mentioned as something that existed, but never explored or explained in depth.

Key syndicators such as Ziv Productions are entirely ignored and syndication is not even given its own paragraph until late in the book, describing the changes in television's structure in the 1980s that foregrounded syndication as the key to programming profit. Similarly, most of the programs that are touched on in the course of the book are prime-time entertainment programming, most of which are still circulating in re-runs. The few mentions of public affairs programming again foreground the networks and programming that has endured over time (such as NBC's *Today* show). In terms of their account of programming, 1950s television appears in *Stay Tuned* much as it looks to 1990s viewers through re-runs seen in syndication, on Nick at Nite, and on other cable outlets.

This resemblance between Sterling and Kittross' (as well as other historians') historiographical image of the 1950s and the currently available re-runs of 1950s television is quite significant. It suggests that historians' views of the past stem from, at least partly, currently circulating visions and myths of that past. While this is not a radical concept, it does have direct impact on historiographical practice: if a particular element of the past does not linger into the present, it is more likely to be ignored in historical works than those that have continued resonance. Some might suggest that this is just and proper, as historians have the benefit of hindsight to see what has become important from the past and this hindsight should be employed to explore the 'important' histories more thoroughly than those which disappeared through a Darwinian model of selection. But this argument is deeply flawed: just because a program such as *Leave it to Beaver* continues to have resonance and circulation in contemporary culture does not mean, as I have discussed above, that it had similar meanings or significance during the era from which it hails. Lawrence Levine, in discussing the tendency to view Shakespeare historically using the same categories and preconceptions associated with the playwright's work today, identifies this trend as 'the historical fallacy of reading the present into the past'.[29] Thus while no one would argue that *I Love Lucy* was not a key cultural text in 1952, it is important to realise that the meanings that we associate with the program today are quite different from those circulating around the show in the 1950s.

Sterling and Kittross' historical account of 1950s television stems from this historical fallacy of reading their present into the past. This affects not only their selection of programming content but their emphasis on network dominance, their foregrounding of 30- and 60-minute programming, and their exclusion of syndication as a key realm of new programming material, all visions that mirror contemporary television broadcasting.[30] They seem to exemplify the axiom that 'history is written by the victors' by foregrounding what remains visible today over what has disappeared over time. Barnouw falls victim to this syndrome less than Sterling and Kittross do, but he is not totally immune. While he does often rely on examples of programming that have not maintained prominence in current culture – such as his comparatively in-depth analysis of *Man Against Crime* as a typical series – and he acknowledges the importance of syndicated entertainment programming, Barnouw's focus on political and public affairs programming ignores the role of syndicated or locally produced shows. This lack is more forgivable in Barnouw's case, as he self-consciously selects examples that he views as either typical or specially noteworthy throughout his narrative. He marginalises the role of programs like *Industry on Parade* as much as Sterling and Kittross do, but his less comprehensive claims and approach partially excuse his gaps and omissions.

The second type of history that I examined is what I term 'selective investigation'. In this type of historical work, the author does not attempt to tell an extended narrative of the past, but rather is interested in probing a specific area of history in depth. These histories tend to foreground the work of previous historians which either left open a gap in scholarship or have glossed over certain complexities or occurrences that this new project endeavours to correct. There is usually a central thesis or argument which serves as a corrective or addendum to other historical works, and the entire historiographical project is framed by this approach and scope. Obviously the tone of such a work is quite different and as such, we must have different expectations for the inclusions and exclusions of this type of history based on its thesis; for example, a hypothetical history examining syndication practices during the 1950s would be more at fault for excluding *Industry on Parade* than a history exploring the

relationship between film studios and television networks. Nevertheless, many selective investigations do offer opportunities to examine the historiographical practices that have led to *Industry on Parade*'s exclusion, and as such they must be addressed here.

The choice of topics for these selective investigations is one realm of historiographical practice that demands scrutiny. While there is a great range of historical work that examines issues in 1950s television, only a few basic types of investigations have appeared in book form. One central type of historical work about this era that has flourished concerns gender and family roles, especially in the domestic sitcom, which emerged as a popular generic form during the 1950s. Lynn Spigel, Nina Leibman, Mary Beth Haralovich, and George Lipsitz all look closely at the circulation of gender discourses on 1950s television by emphasising network, prime-time domestic sitcoms.[31] Although these inquiries are often quite exceptional and enlightening, they do not recognise the roles that programs in other genres, time slots, or distribution formats might have played to support or contradict their theses; again, this is suggestive of my discussion above on *Industry on Parade*'s gender representations versus the *Leave it to Beaver* myth. While I do not wish to suggest that any of these historical endeavours must attempt to be all-inclusive or comprehensive, there must be an acknowledgement of the absences that are structured into these works and how the assumptions that guide many of these histories may be propelled by Levine's historical fallacy of reading the present into the past.

Another thematic category of specific investigations surrounds the television industry. William Boddy, Michele Hilmes, and Christopher Anderson all have works (at least partially) dedicated to exploring the television industry during this era.[32] Boddy mostly ignores syndication and programming issues, but both Hilmes and Anderson give detailed considerations of specific programs as related to the intersection of the film and television (and radio in Hilmes' case) industries as well as in-depth discussions of syndication, focusing on Hollywood programming and films. While again none of these historians acknowledge *Industry on Parade* or other public affairs programs, it is consistent with the stated goals of Hilmes and Anderson to focus on the syndication of Hollywood products, not on the other forms of syndication active during this era. At least within these latter two histories, television during the 1950s does not appear to be the domain solely of network prime-time programming; they consider syndicated programming, films on television, special events, and other variants of non-network prime-time programming.

Despite the openings within Hilmes and Anderson's works, there is still a lack of historical work non-network and non-prime-time programming. A 1994 issue of *The Velvet Light Trap* on 'Television Histories' typifies the range of historical work being done on television.[33] One piece explores the frequently visited neighbourhood of 1950s domestic sitcoms ('What Ozzie Did for a Living' by Tinky 'Dakota' Weisblat) and another approaches gender issues employing the theoretical paradigm of using the 'star' as the central historical focal point ('The Face on the Lunch Box' by Gael Sweeny). Two other industry-centred articles concentrate on early network practice, focusing on both a failed network ('A Failed Vision: The Mutual Television Network' by James Schwoch) and the most successful network ('NBC Program Clearance Policies during the 1950s' by Matthew Murray). Only one of the five articles, 'Televising Postwar Los Angeles' by Mark Williams, considers non-network programming. This essay explores a local Los Angeles public affairs program, *City at Night*, broadcast in 1949 on KTLA. While Williams' specific analysis of the program is not relevant to a study of *Industry on Parade*, his methodological assertions bear directly on this project, suggesting that 'work on local television can suggest discontinuities to pervasive network-centred television histories,... [emphasising] the potential value of further historical work in television at the local level, the level at which all television is experienced'.[34] Although *Industry on Parade* is not specifically local, historical exploration of syndicated programming can similarly point to fissures in the seemingly solid edifice of predominant network-centred histories.

Throughout my discussion of selective investigation historiography, I have shown how often issues concerning syndicated, public affairs, and non-prime-time programming have all been marginalised. I do not wish to suggest that the reason for

this habitual oversight is that the historians mentioned above are ignorant of these other forms of programming. Clearly most broadcast historians have a solid knowledge of the various programming forms and modes of distribution practices throughout broadcast history. If so, what other reasons might be factors in the consistent lack of attention paid to this type of programming? One key reason concerns lack of access. To write about the texts of *I Love Lucy* or *The Honeymooners* requires only a TV, a VCR, and the right cable stations or video rental stores. A program like *Industry on Parade* is available in archives, but this is clearly not as convenient as home viewing and taping.

Another potential obstacle blocking more writing on programs such as *Industry on Parade* is lack of specific knowledge. Most historians know few specific forms of the practices of syndicated or fifteen-minute programming. This is obviously a self-perpetuating cycle – because *Industry on Parade* and its like are absent from histories, future historians do not learn about them and are thus less likely to examine these programs themselves. The one site of historical dissemination which does contain information on *Industry on Parade* is the programming reference book, such as *Total Television*.[35] Though guidebooks do include the program in their listings, their information is minimal and somewhat inaccurate: for example, *Total Television* lists *Industry on Parade* run dates from 1950 through 1958, not its actual farewell in 1960. Although this is not the most critical of errors, there is little in the description or associated information to inspire a historian toward further pursuit of this program.

The final reason why I believe programs such as *Industry on Parade* have been given short historical shrift concerns the specific work of the historian. As any historian must labour to choose a topic, research it, and turn it into a coherent and compelling historical project, the topic must have some core motivating factor. This helps explain the number of historical works that consider the role of gender in society (including my own here) – as gender power relations have an impact on all members of our culture, it makes sense that many historians, especially but not exclusively women, would devote intensive labour toward understanding, re-evaluating, and undermining dominant structures of gender. Much of the critical and historical work done around television has laboured to bring respect to an object and field of study which is often regarded as inconsequential or potentially damaging to society. Histories of broadcasting policy often call into question the assumptions and power structures that have brought the status quo into being, and they work to undo or replace these past injustices. Many selective investigations look to correct the injustices of previous histories, to demarginalise the victims of past historiographical practice, be they radio amateurs or African-American inventors. All of these examples suggest projects that a particular historian can be moved and inspired by, spurring and motivating their practice.

Just as a topic must inspire a historian to produce history, it must also be able to be circulated within academic discourse. The contemporary scholarly situation is a marketplace where the historian produces a history to be sold (as a book or an article) or bartered (at a conference, for the exchange of other insights). As such, the historian must produce a history that produces sufficient interest from other historians to make it marketable. Many histories are written following contemporary trends and styles of the field; thus particular approaches (e.g. gender analyses, industrial histories) may be written more often because they are a proven commodity, while a more arcane or obscure topic may go ignored for fear of publishing (or tenure) rejections. This may appear cynical, but it is a crucial concern in the perennially tight academic job market. It is a dated myth to believe that history stems solely from the pursuit of the truth; while historians may work to satisfy their own and others' craving for knowledge of the past, if that knowledge cannot successfully thrive within the academic marketplace, the topic will probably remain unexplored.

Given the dual requirements of historiographical and marketplace motivation, it is not surprising that a text such as *Industry on Parade* would be ignored by most historians. With its huge repertoire of program reels, mostly depicting a surface gloss of the manufacturing of products such as cheese and electrical insulation, the program quickly becomes quite boring. While there are a number of gems within the 500+ episodes, for every 'Mrs America Serves Again!' there are 25 segments such as 'The Big Lift!' (manufacturing industrial tongs), 'Business

Office Magician!' (manufacturing cash registers and adding machines), or 'Decreasing Danger!' (outlining factory safety programs). An historian might soon tire of watching these reels of industrial supremacy. Similarly, a reader of such a history may not have more than a passing interest in the topic and as such, a publisher would be unlikely to give a scholar an advance to write the history of *Industry on Parade* or of syndicated public affairs programming in the 1950s.

Despite this, I am writing a history of *Industry on Parade*. I watched many episodes of the program and researched its production and exhibition processes. But I would not be writing a history of this program were it not for the corresponding historiography of the program, as these are the key issues that have inspired and motivated my work (and made me believe that the project might have life within the academic marketplace of publication). Likewise, I did not watch multiple episodes of *Industry on Parade* for the knowledge of the contents of the program, but rather as part of an internship at the Archives Center of the NMAH. Through this internship, I tried to explore all aspects of the archival process and consider how the archiving of a program such as *Industry on Parade* impacts historiographical practices. I will now turn to these archival and historiographical practices to consider how my own and future histories are determined and impacted by these archival processes.

When I took an internship at the NMAH Archives Center for the summer of 1995, audio-visual archivist Wendy Shay mentioned a number of projects for which a committed individual was needed. One of these was the *Industry on Parade* collection. When Shay first described the program to me, I was less than excited by the prospect of viewing hours of industrial newsreel footage, but she conveyed the importance that the film reels be properly archived and noted that this was the only available project that was directly related to television history, my area of interest. Additionally, most of my work would be focused on the physical storage and repair of the reels of film, a task that does not concern the content of the film. As the internship progressed, Shay and I discovered crucial work that needed to be done regarding the collection's content, as attention had to be paid to the archival

INDUSTRY ON PARADE

A brand new look at our America

PEABODY AWARD WINNER

WEEKLY TV FEATURE NEWSREEL

REEL NO. 331

ANN ARBOR, Mich. On a roof-top laboratory of the University of Michigan, a device known as an 'integrating sphere' is used to measure the light transmitted by a glass block--part of a research program aimed at improving the natural illumination of our homes and classrooms, factories and shops. This Daylighting Laboratory, financed by Owens-Illinois Glass Company, has found that by changing the angles of ribs on the faces and interior surfaces of hollow glass blocks, it's possible to direct controlled quantities of light into a room and to distribute that light more uniformly. Low angled rays of a winter sun can be directed into a room, while the hot glare of a summer sun can be rejected. The methods proved and perfected in the laboratory are shown put into practice in a strikingly modern house, making the best possible use of the daylight that man has admitted into his dwellings for many centuries.

TILLAMOOK, Oregon In a giant aircraft hangar, where Navy blimps took off in search of enemy submaries during World War II, the Diamond Lumber Company has set up a mill to convert much of the region's abundant supply of timber into plywood. Beneath the soaring ceiling there's enough room for the mill and a whole freight train as well, enabling the product to be loaded for shipment out of the weather. And by leasing the hangar from the county, which received it from the Navy after the war, the company provides savings for local taxpayers as well as wages for those it employs.

Fig. 3. A portion of the original 'informational insert' accompanying one reel of *Industry of Parade*. [Archives Center, Smithsonian Institution, National Museum of American History]

document most taken for granted in historical practice: the finding aid.

Within any archival collection, be it composed of papers, photographs, or film reels, the finding aid is the sole interface between a researcher and the archived material. The finding aid allows the researcher to glean what material will be contained within the archival collection without going through the tedious (and often damaging) process of manually sifting through the collection. If a particular topic or issue is not contained within the finding aid, it becomes difficult for the researcher to discover this information within the archival collection. An example of this process is my own archival research for this paper at the Wisconsin Center for Film and Theater Research. I knew that NBC and NAM had some relationship concerning *Industry on Parade*,

but did not know the details of this arrangement. I searched the finding aid for references to *Industry on Parade*, NAM, Arthur Lodge, and Johnny Johnstone (both of whose names appeared in the NMAH collection repeatedly) to no avail. It was only after I discovered the name Frank McCall in an article from *Business Week* that I was able to discover the relative wealth of information about *Industry on Parade* within the NBC collection. With no other leads to finding clues within the finding aid, there is little way for me to know whether the hundreds of boxes of NBC papers contain more information about the program (such as the exact processes involved in NBC ceasing production of the show) without haphazardly searching through random papers for minute references. As such, a finding aid is a key historiographical document, often delimiting and determining the scope of a historian's project.

The finding aid for the *Industry on Parade* collection at NMAH was a work-in-progress when I arrived at the Archives Center. The document available for researchers to search the collection was actually more of a temporary 'catalogue' than a full-fledged finding aid, providing a brief introduction to the program, which contains some factual inaccuracies and vague descriptions, followed by a lengthy catalogue of episodes, briefly listing the contents of each film reel. The episode guide was quite difficult to use, as it merely listed the reel number (with no air date), the title of each segment, and one phrase describing the segment, usually identifying the company, location, and industrial process portrayed in the segment. While the information included is potentially quite useful, there is neither a subject index nor a table of contents to cross-reference episodes. Additionally, many of the descriptions are highly inaccurate, missing key contents or containing misinformation. The lack of a true finding aid and the flaws of the catalogue stem from the process by which *Industry on Parade* entered the Smithsonian Institution's archival collections.

NAM donated the *Industry on Parade* collection, consisting of 428 film reels,[36] to the Smithsonian in 1974. At that time, the Archives Center at the NMAH did not exist;[37] it was determined, by what was known as the National Museum of History and Technology at the time, that the collection should be housed in the Division of Agriculture and Natural Resources (DANR) because the content of the program concerned industry and technology, an area of specialty of the DANR. Film archiving was a relatively obscure practice in the mid-1970s, and as such the archivists at the DANR did the best they could with the collection with no proper training or knowledge of film archival practice. In order to make the collection accessible to interested researchers, the archivists viewed each episode and took notes on its contents to create the catalogue. Many of the episode descriptions enclosed with the reels were discarded in this process. As such, the catalogue was based solely on the viewing notes, leading to an inconsistent document containing misinterpretations and incomplete information. As procedures for standard film preservation were not readily available in this era, the films were stored on improper reels and in cardboard mailers until the NMAH transferred the collection to the Archives Center in 1994.

Although I do not wish to blame the staff of DANR for mishandling the collection, this type of treatment is indicative of the strange place that television history has within the institutional structure of museums and archives. While many archivists and curators have graduate education in their area of specialty, most moving-image archivists or television history curators have little formal training in media history and archiving. Until 1996, there were no formal programs of study for moving-image archiving in the United States and media studies is a still developing field within this country. The need for moving-image archives has grown more quickly than the educational system's ability to train archivists, and as such, the system for archiving moving-image material is less formal and institutionalised than many museum and library practices. Most moving-image archivists come from diverse backgrounds and learn their trade through apprenticeships, practice, and an active and cooperative professional society, the Association of Moving Image Archivists. Just as television studies as a field is less defined and formally structured than most disciplines, the archiving of television history overlaps with a variety of disciplinary and institutional structures and thus has less stability than traditional archival areas.

My primary project as an archival intern was to transfer the film stock to proper archival cores and canisters, repairing damaged segments along the way. Given that the film stock was in poor condition and that the Archives Center has only one Steenbeck film viewing machine, the goal was to transfer all footage to reference video copies which would be available for researchers to view in the Center. This is obviously an expensive process and given the lack of budgetary priority allocated to archives in general, the video transfer project was on the backburner. This project was caught in a typical paradox: the Smithsonian will internally grant money to archival projects that have demonstrated significant outside research interest, but as the *Industry on Parade* collection has been nearly inaccessible to researchers for years, it is difficult to demonstrate significant interest. The video transfers had been done occasionally as necessary for research projects with a small budget allocation; thus there were approximately 30 scattered episodes available on reference video for researchers to view in the Center.

As I was working on the project, I discovered many of the inaccuracies in the catalogue. Shay encouraged me to supplement my work on the physical film storage with research to correct the catalogue and work to expand it into a full finding aid. I discovered that the Library of Congress (LOC) has a fairly large collection of *Industry on Parade* episodes as well and that they have collected in a bound volume the informational inserts from the film reels, detailing episode contents and subject matter. I began cross-referencing the NMAH catalogue with the LOC volume to incorporate air dates, accurate information, and important contents that the DANR had missed. Since I left the NMAH, the corrected catalogue has been scanned into a word processor and is being edited with the intention of making it accessible for researchers to search via computer. When I edited the catalogue, I selected and indicated which episode segments would be useful to researchers investigating issues of gender, ethnicity, and disabilities, three topics that were addressed, explicitly or implicitly, in *Industry on Parade* segments and that correspond to current interests in cultural history; these topics will eventually be cross-referenced for researchers who are searching the Archives Center collection. Obviously there were many other issues that I could have highlighted, but this is one of the key ways in which the creation of a finding aid can help shape and mold the historiographical work that is practiced upon a given archival collection.

Throughout this project I have attempted to highlight key issues in historiography that are brought to light through an examination of *Industry on Parade*. Cultural and media historians must engage in this type of careful investigation of other historians' practices, consideration of the issues raised by the topic of one's own history, and, most of all, an in-depth examination of how one's own historiographical practice has been delimited by research material that itself contains selections, inclusions, and omissions. Key to this process is an attempt to acknowledge that no historical document, be it a reel of film footage, a magazine article,

or an archival finding aid, is outside of discursive production and power relations. As such, one cannot look to any traces of the past as transparent gateways to the 'truth' of that past. My case study of *Industry on Parade* points to how historiographical practices are not easy to predict based on dominant power relations: that which is historiographically marginalised may be culturally dominant and hegemonic. Likewise, that which may appear to be a boring, monovocal and simplistic text may contain a more heterogeneous and varied set of discourses than visible at first glance. As such we must widen our histories to include examples of texts that have been previously excluded and ignored, whether they be marginal examples of counter-cultural knowledge or hegemonic capitalist propaganda. ♣

Acknowledgement

I would like to thank Michele Hilmes, Vance Kepley, Mark Langer, Rick Prelinger, Jennifer Wang, and an anonymous reader for their helpful comments regarding this paper and my research process, John Fleckner and the Archives Center at the National Museum of American History for the opportunity to work on this project, and Wendy Shay, whose guidance, feedback, and encouragement are responsible for both this project and the archiving of *Industry on Parade*.

Notes

1. Although it may seem odd for a paper concerned with historiography, most of the information explored in this paper does not feature detailed footnoting and chronicling of sources. This is primarily because of the key role that my own personal experiences, archiving the program at the National Museum of American History Archives Center during the summer of 1995, served in researching this topic; when not otherwise noted, information included in this paper was discovered during that practice and can mostly be rediscovered within that collection.

2. NAM promotional material quoted in Elizabeth A. Fones-Wolf, *Selling Free Enterprise: The Business Assault on Labor and Liberalism, 1945–60* (Urbana: University of Illinois Press, 1994), 52. *Industry on Parade* is an example of the genre of sponsored documentary films that, while being

plentiful in number, have been vastly underexamined by scholars. While it may be the longest running and most critically-acclaimed example of this genre, there were other television programs, radio broadcasts, and films made to promote various organisational, industrial and governmental perspectives and agendas. These films and broadcasts have long been considered 'ephemera' and ignored by most scholars, though Rick Prelinger's commitment to archiving and circulating these texts through videotapes and CD-ROMs has led to greater knowledge of sponsored films; this public availability seemingly has not triggered substantial scholarly writings on the topic. Fones-Wolf's history of the public relations efforts of American industry during this era is an exception to this general lack of scholarly material; her book provides a detailed context for NAM's role within labour and corporate history.

3. Fones-Wolf, 41.

4. Letter from Earl Bunting, managing director of National Association of Manufacturers, to Joseph McConnell, president of National Broadcasting Company (18 December 1950). Papers of Francis McCall, NBC Collection.

5. Ibid.

6. 'Industry on Parade', TV Guide (27 July 1957): 22.

7. Letter from Bunting, NBC Collection.

8. TV Guide (28 January 1956), Wisconsin Edition; my use of Wisconsin as exemplary material stems solely from my access to local Wisconsin documents, not because of any knowledge of Wisconsin being a typical or special case in terms of syndicated programming.

9. Letter from Bunting, NBC Collection.

10. 'TV Programs This Week', New York Times (17 April 1955): 15.

11. TV Guide.

12. NBC Program Schedules, Papers of Francis McCall, NBC Collection.

13. 'NAM Scores a Hit on TV – Soft-Pedaling Commercials', Business Week (19 April 1952): 86.

14. Further research into this area would certainly lead to the Hagley Museum and Library, Wilmington, DE, which contains NAM's corporate papers; whether this includes viewer mail concerning Industry on Parade is unknown but certainly worth further examination.

15. 'NAM Scores a Hit on TV', 88.

16. Fones-Wolf, 204.

17. All of the titles of Industry on Parade segments highlight the energy and vitality of American industry through their hyperbolic usage of exclamation marks.

18. Unless otherwise noted, textual references stem from episode 18, viewed at NMAH.

19. Keith Jenkins, Re-Thinking History (London: Routledge, 1991), 49.

20. Joanne Meyerowitz, 'Introduction: Women and Gender in Postwar America, 1945–60', in Not June Cleaver, ed. Joanne Meyerowitz (Philadelphia: Temple University Press, 1994), 1–2, and Stephanie Coontz, The Way We Never Were (New York: Basic Books, 1992), especially chapter 2 entitled '"Leave It to Beaver" and "Ozzie and Harriet": American Families in the 1950s', 23–41.

21. Coontz, 160–162, and Joanne Meyerowitz, 'Beyond the Feminine Mystique: A Reassessment of Postwar Mass Culture, 1946–58', in Meyerowitz, 229–262. Meyerowitz specifically questions and contradicts Betty Friedan's assertions, made in The Feminine Mystique, that mass culture denies any women's roles except for domestic wife and mother.

22. For some examples of more nuanced and varied analyses of gender on television in the 1950s, see Lynn Spigel, Make Room for TV (Chicago: University of Chicago Press, 1992); Lisa Parks, 'Watching the "Working Gals": 1950s Sitcoms and the Social Repositioning of Women and the Postwar Era', Console-ing Passions Conference (April 1994), Tucson, AZ; and Tasha Oren, 'Looking Back on a Near-Perfect Future', Console-ing Passions Conference (April 1996), Madison, WI.

23. Industry on Parade claims that female employment had reached nine per cent in 1950 while Coontz gives a figure around 20 per cent, but as the NAM number is given in passing by the announcer, it is difficult to assess exactly what they claimed to be measuring or from what source the statistic derived.

24. For a detailed discussion of women in the workplace in 1950s sitcoms, including Private Secretary, see Parks, 'Watching the "Working Gals"'.

25. The one mention of Industry on Parade within a scholarly history that I discovered was found in Fones-Wolf's book on corporate public relations history during this era – television, film, and radio programming are all mentioned and discussed in her book, but it is not primarily a media history text.

26. Christopher H. Sterling and John M. Kittross, Stay Tuned, 2nd edn. (Belmont, CA: Wadsworth Publishing Company, 1990), Erik Barnouw, The Golden

Web (New York: Oxford University Press, 1968), and Barnouw, *The Image Empire* (New York: Oxford University Press, 1970). I am only using the latter two volumes of Barnouw's text as they correspond with the time period of *Industry on Parade.*

27. Sterling and Kittross, vii.

28. Barnouw, 1968, 4.

29. Lawrence W. Levine, *Highbrow/Lowbrow* (Cambridge: Harvard University Press, 1988), 31.

30. Syndication is currently an active arena of new programming, but attached to this recent boom in syndicated original programming is the myth that this a new development that emerged in the late-1980s, a myth that *Stay Tuned* helps perpetuate.

31. See Spigel, Nina C. Leibman, *Living Room Lectures* (Austin: University of Texas Press, 1995), Mary Beth Haralovich, 'Sit-coms and Suburbs: Positioning the 1950s Homemaker', in *Private Screenings*, ed. Lynn Spigel and Denise Mann (Minneapolis: University of Minnesota Press, 1992), 111–142, and George Lipsitz, 'Why Remember Mama? The Changing Face of a Woman's Narrative', in *Time Passages* (Minneapolis: University of Minnesota Press, 1990), 77–98.

32. See William Boddy, *Fifties Television* (Urbana: University of Illinois Press, 1990), Michele Hilmes, *Hollywood and Broadcasting* (Urbana: University of Illinois Press, 1990), and Christopher Anderson, *Hollywood TV* (Austin: University of Texas Press, 1994).

33. *The Velvet Light Trap* 33, special issue 'Television Histories' (Spring, 1994).

34. Mark Williams, 'Televising Postwar Los Angeles: "Remote" Possibilities in a "City at Night"', *The Velvet Light Trap* 33 (Spring, 1994): 35.

35. See Alex McNeil, *Total Television*, 3rd ed. (New York: Penguin, 1991) and Hal Erickson, *Syndicated Television: The First Forty Years, 1947–87* (Jefferson, NC: McFarland & Co., 1989), 87–88.

36. The collection is missing a number of the over 500 episodes in the series, though the Smithsonian has the most comprehensive collection of the program to be found in accessible archives.

37. The Archives Center was founded in 1982 as primarily a print and photographic archive, although it now archives all media and formats together, unusual for most archives.

Bibliography

Anderson, Christopher. *Hollywood TV* (Austin: University of Texas Press, 1994).

Barnouw, Erik. *The Golden Web* (New York: Oxford University Press, 1968).

Barnouw, Erik. *The Image Empire* (New York: Oxford University Press, 1970).

Boddy, William. *Fifties Television* (Urbana: University of Illinois Press, 1990).

Coontz, Stephanie. *The Way We Never Were* (New York: Basic Books, 1992).

Erickson, Hal. *Syndicated Television: The First Forty Years, 1947–87.* (Jefferson, NC: McFarland & Co., 1989), 87–88.

Fones-Wolf, Elizabeth A. *Selling Free Enterprise: The Business Assault on Labor and Liberalism, 1945–60.* (Urbana: University of Illinois Press, 1994).

Haralovich, Mary Beth. 'Sit-coms and Suburbs: Positioning the 1950s Homemaker'. In *Private Screenings*, ed., Lynn Spigel and Denise Mann (Minneapolis: University of Minnesota Press, 1992), 111–142.

Hilmes, Michele. *Hollywood and Broadcasting* (Urbana: University of Illinois Press, 1990).

Industry on Parade. TV Guide (27 July 1957): 22–23.

Industry on Parade Collection, Smithsonian Institution, National Museum of American History, Archives Center, Washington, DC. (NMAH)

Industry on Parade Episode Guide, Library of Congress, Motion Pictures and Sound Division, Washington, DC. (LOC)

Jenkins, Keith. *Re-Thinking History* (London: Routledge, 1991).

Leibman, Nina C. *Living Room Lectures* (Austin: University of Texas Press, 1995).

Levine, Lawrence W. *Highbrow/Lowbrow* (Cambridge: Harvard University Press, 1988).

Lipsitz, George. 'The Meaning of Memory: Family, Class, and Ethnicity in Early Network Television' and 'Why Remember Mama? The Changing Face of a Woman's Narrative.' In *Time Passages* (Minneapolis: University of Minnesota Press, 1990), 39–98.

McNeil, Alex. *Total Television*, 3rd edn. (New York: Penguin, 1991).

Meyerowitz, Joanne. 'Introduction: Women and Gender in Postwar America, 1945–60' and 'Beyond the Feminine Mystique: A Reassessment of Postwar Mass Culture, 1946–58'. In *Not June Cleaver*, ed. Joanne Meyerowitz (Philadelphia: Temple University Press, 1994), 1–18, 229–262.

'NAM Scores a Hit on TV – Soft-Pedaling Commercials'. *Business Week* (19 April 1952): 86–88.

National Broadcasting Company Collection, Papers of Francis C. McCall, 1951–52, Boxes 309–311, State Historical Society of Wisconsin. (NBC)

Parks, Lisa. 'Watching the "Working Gals": 1950s Sitcoms and the Social Repositioning of Women and the Postwar Era.' Console-ing Passions Conference, April 1994, Tucson, AZ.

Spigel, Lynn. *Make Room for TV* (Chicago: University of Chicago Press, 1992).

Sterling, Christopher H. and John M. Kittross. *Stay Tuned*, 2nd ed. (Belmont, CA: Wadsworth Publishing Company, 1990).

TV Guide (28 January 1956), Wisconsin Edition.

'TV Programs This Week'. *New York Times* (17 April 1955): 15.

The Velvet Light Trap 33, special issue 'Television Histories' (Spring, 1994).

Williams, Mark. 'Televising Postwar Los Angeles: "Remote" Possibilities in a "City at Night".' *The Velvet Light Trap* 33 (Spring, 1994): 24–36.

The Casablanca File
Colin McArthur

Hon. professor at Queen Margaret College, Edinburgh, and Founder and Director of its Centre for Scottish Popular Culture.

Television and magazine advertisments; film and television plays; the names of night clubs; bars and restaurants; the routines of stage and television comedians; titles of books; sub-editors' headlines; even exchanges of personal conversation. **Casablanca** figures in all of them and in a great deal else. **Casablanca** is perhaps the most prolific generator of secondary texts in the field of popular culture. In language semiotics, **Casablanca** is profoundly intertextual. A archeological task of recovering the most important meaning that the hegemony of romantic nostalgia suppresses – **Casablanca's** demand that the moral choices be made in the face of fascism.

Available from:
John Libbey & Company Pty Ltd, Level 10, 15–17 Young Street, Sydney NSW 2000 Australia

Ph: +61 (0)2 9251 4099
Fax: +61 (0)2 9251 4428
E-mail: jlsydney@mpx.com.au

ISBN 0 86196 457 8

Softcover	AUD$23.00	48 pp.
Airmail	AUD$8.00	
Surfacemail	AUD$5.00	

UPCOMING ISSUES/ CALL FOR PAPERS

Film History 9, 3
Sreenwriters and Screenwriting
   edited by John Belton

Film History 9, 4
International Cinema of the Teens
   edited by Kristin Thompson

Film History 10, 1
Cinema Pioneers
   edited by Stephen Bottomore
   (deadline for submissions
   1 September 1997)

Film History 10, 2
Film and Television
   edited by Richard Koszarski
   (deadline for submissions
   1 December 1997)

Film History 10, 3
Red Scare
   edited by Daniel J. Leab
   (deadline for submissions
   1 March1998)

Film History 10, 4
Special issue on the Centennial of Cinema Literature

Film History 11, 1
Film Technology
   edited by John Belton
   (deadline for submissions
   1 September 1998)

The editors of *FILM HISTORY* encourage the submission of manuscripts within the overall scope of the journal. These may correspond to the announced themes of future issues above, but may equally be on any topic relevant to film history.

Back issues of Film History – volumes 1–9 (1987–97)

FILM HISTORY

*Back issue and
subscription order form*

PLEASE SUPPLY:

.... Subscription(s) to *Film History*
        at Institutional/Private rate (please specify)
        Surface/Air Mail (please specify)
.... Back issues of the following volumes/issues
....
....
I enclose payment of £/US$ ....
Please send me a Pro-forma invoice for: £/US$ ....

Please debit my Access/Master Card/Visa/
American Express/Diner's Club credit card:
Account no..Expiry..........
Name ....
Address ....
....
....
.... Zip/Postcode ....

Signature ....Date ....
(This form may be photocopied)

SUBSCRIPTION RATES & BACK ISSUE PRICES
Institutional Subscription rates:
   All countries (except N. America)
   Surface mail   £85/A$170
   Air mail   £95/A$190
   N. America
   Surface mail   US$151   Air mail   US$172
*Private Subscription rates (subscribers warrant that
copies are for their PERSONAL use only):*
   All countries (except N. America)
   Surface mail   £33/A$66
   Air mail   £44/A$88
   N. America
   Surface mail   US$59   Air mail   US$79
Back issues: All issues available – Volumes 1 to 8:
£12/US$20/A$24 each number.

JOHN LIBBEY & COMPANY LTD,
Level 10, 15–17 Young Street
Sydney, NSW 2000, Australia
Telephone: **+61 (0)2 9251 4099**
Fax: **+61 (0)2 9251 4428**
E-mail: **jlsydney@mpx.com.au**

FILM HISTORY

An International Journal

Aims and Scope

The subject of *Film History* is the historical
development of the motion picture, and the social,
technological and economic context in which this
has occurred. Its areas of interest range from the
technical and entrepreneurial innovations of early
and pre-cinema experiments, through all aspects
of the production, distribution, exhibition and
reception of commercial and non-commercial
motion pictures.

In addition to original research in these areas, the
journal will survey the paper and film holdings of
archives and libraries worldwide, publish selected
examples of primary documentation (such as early
film scenarios) and report on current publications,
exhibitions, conferences and research in progress.
Many future issues will be devoted to
comprehensive studies of single themes.

Instructions to Authors

Manuscripts will be accepted with the
understanding that their content is unpublished
and is not being submitted for publication
elsewhere. If any part of the paper has been
previously published, or is to be published
elsewhere, the author must include this information
at the time of submittal. Manuscripts should be
sent to the Editor-in-Chief:

   Richard Koszarski
   Box TEN
   Teaneck, New Jersey, 07666, USA
   E-mail: filmhist@aol.com

excepting for submissions to thematic issues
directed by one of the Associate Editors.

The publishers will do everything possible to
ensure prompt publication, therefore it is required
that each submitted manuscript be in complete
form. Please take the time to check all references,
figures, tables and text for errors before
submission.